And the TWO Become ONE

Building a Blissful Union Not Easily Broken

And the TWO Become ONE

Building a Blissful Union Not Easily Broken

SHARLENE FULLWOOD

AND THE TWO BECOME ONE by Dr. Sharlene F. Fullwood
Published by Creation House
A Charisma Media Company
600 Rinehart Road
Lake Mary, Florida 32746
www.charismamedia.com

Unless otherwise noted, Scripture quotations are from the New King James Version of the Bible. Copyright © 1979, 1980, 1982 by Thomas Nelson, Inc., publishers. Used by permission.

Scripture quotations marked KJV are from the King James Version of the Bible.

All definitions taken from the American Dictionary of The English Language, Noah Webster (New York: S. Converse, 1828). Copyright @ 1995, 1993, 1989, 1987, 1985, 1983, 1980 by the Foundation for American Christian Education San Francisco, California.

Design Director: Bill Johnson
Cover design by Terry Clifton

Visit the author by e-mail: sharlenefullwood@comcast.net

Library of Congress Cataloging in Publication Data: 2012937829
International Standard Book Number: 978-1-61638-977-2
E-book International Standard Book Number: 978-1-61638-978-9

While the author has made every effort to provide accurate telephone numbers and Internet addresses at the time of publication, neither the publisher nor the author assumes any responsibility for errors or for changes that occur after publication.

First edition

12 13 14 15 16 — 9 8 7 6 5 4 3 2 1
Printed in the United States of America

DEDICATION

To God be the glory!

TABLE OF CONTENTS

INTRODUCTION

Marriage was instituted by God. Man and woman were created to be companions to one another. They were to cohabitate, procreate, love one another, and fulfill kingdom purpose personally and as a union.

> So God created man in His own image; in the image of God He created him; male and female He created them. Then God blessed them, and God said to them, "Be fruitful and multiply; fill the earth and subdue it; have dominion over the fish of the sea, over the birds of the air, and over every living thing that moves on the earth."
>
> —Genesis 1:27–28

The marriage union is important to God yet we see how divorce is rampant in the world today. Couples are treating this union like a temporary arrangement. Marriage is being taken lightly with the attitude of it being a "trial run," and if it doesn't work, divorce is a prevalent option. Unfortunately, this mind-set has caused divorce rates to soar in the secular world as well as the church world.

This book is being written with the author's intent to

give sound doctrine out of the Word of God on the major topics that impact the marital union. The author is coming from a Christian viewpoint and dealing with topics that are sometimes not taught in a "church" setting for couples. Nonetheless, this teaching is relevant Bible-based information to assist couples in navigating through situations that arise in the marital relationship. The book is written in wisdom and based on godly principles. Know that all the teaching is directly from a biblical standpoint, but it is probably not being taught with the "usual" conservative Christian viewpoint. All teachings are expounded upon using Matthew 7:12 as the foundation principle: "Therefore, whatever you want men to do to you, do also to them, for this is the Law and the Prophets." This principle is known as the "golden rule," and I believe it behooves all to honor this rule so that we remember to treat one another with respect and love.

The information will minister to you and your mate whether you're a newlywed or a veteran in marriage. It will be informative whether your marriage is still in a state of happiness and bliss or it's begun or settling in stagnation and facing issues. As you read this book, please keep an open mind and be willing to change the way you view your mate and your marriage. Be willing to make the necessary changes in your marriage to take your relationship to a new level of love and intimacy. Marriage can be great if both parties are willing to adapt and work at it. If you're reading this book, hopefully it means you're willing to work and take your marriage from OK to great, from great to greater, from ordinary to extraordinary.

Chapter 1

MARRIAGE IS ORDAINED BY GOD

GENESIS 2:18 READS, "And the Lord God said, 'It is not good that man should be alone; I will make him a helper comparable to him.'" First note that God determined that it wasn't good for man to be alone; therefore, God made him a helpmeet. Understand that when God made Eve, He did not make a subordinate maid for Adam. God did not create Eve to just clean the house, do the laundry, shop for groceries, wash the dishes, have babies, take care of the babies/children, cook meals, and give him some sex when he wanted it; but the Word of the Lord says God made him "a helper comparable to him."

The word *comparable* means someone worthy of comparison. It means someone being of equal regard; someone that may be estimated as equal. In other words, God made female of equal regard to be a companion for man. She was created so that man would not be alone. Woman was created to assist man so that they could work together to fulfill purposes and goals. She was created to cohabitate with man so that they could live cordially together, cooperating together, fulfilling the plan of God together for their lives both personally and jointly as a union. Woman

1

was created so that man would have someone to share his experiences with, his dreams with, his goals with, his life with, and someone to display his love upon. Proverbs 18:22 reads, "He who finds a wife finds a good thing, And obtains favor from the Lord." Men, you found "a good thing."

Understand also that God did not make man just to be a "bread winner," to do the lawn work and take out the trash and perform what are deemed as "manly duties" around the house. Man was not created for the woman to boss around and fulfill "every one" of her sometimes irrational expectations. But rather man/husband and woman/wife are to work together as "one," completing one another, finding satisfaction, happiness, and completion from one another with God being the center of it all. God is to be the center of the husband's life; God is to be the center of the wife's life; and most definitely God is to be the center of the marriage.

Women, you are to love and respect your husband. Men, you are to love and cherish your wife. Men, you have what she needs…God made you that way. Women, you have what he needs…God made you that way. The key is finding out what your mate needs and learning how to release it and give it to your partner so that your union is complete and whole. In order to fulfill this, one needs to be open to learning, changing, and loving unselfishly.

The marriage union is important to God. It is the foundation of the family. In the Bible, God's relationship with His people is illustrated as a marriage to the body of Christ. He's the Bridegroom and the church is the bride. The bride, which is the church, comes from the Bridegroom, which is God/Christ, just as Eve/the bride "came" from Adam/the bridegroom, with God being the Creator and source of it all.

> And the LORD God caused a deep sleep to fall on
> Adam, and he slept; and He took one of his ribs, and
> closed up the flesh in its place. Then the rib which
> the LORD God had taken from man He made into a
> woman, and He brought her to the man.
>
> —GENESIS 2:21–22

God gave man a special gift…woman. Everything that God made is good. Every gift that God gives is good. It's all good. Every gift that God gives to us is to be treasured because it comes from God. You must remember that God is the Creator and source of everything and that He must be kept the "center" of everything, including one's marriage.

> He who has the bride is the bridegroom; but the
> friend of the bridegroom, who stands and hears
> him, rejoices greatly because of the bridegroom's
> voice. Therefore this joy of mine if fulfilled.
>
> —JOHN 3:29

> Then I, John, saw the holy city, New Jerusalem,
> coming down out of heaven from God, prepared as
> a bride adorned for her husband.
>
> —REVELATION 21:2

It was not a coincidence that God made woman (the bride) from man (the bridegroom), even as we the body of Christ (the bride) are made in the image of God, from God by God. God depicts the importance of marriage by the many examples that He uses when teaching that He is the Bridegroom and the body of Christ is the bride. God consistently shows His devotion and love to the church/bride as man is to consistently and selflessly show his devotion and love to his bride/wife. We are taught in the

Word of God that the love is not to be one-sided, but that even as God loves us and shows us His love for us, we His children are to reciprocate the love. This means that the body of Christ/the children of God/the people of God/ God's bride, the church, are to consistently and selflessly show our devotion and love to our bridegroom, God. We are to love and respect God.

This directly correlates and is paralleled to the fact that women are to consistently and selflessly show their love and give their respect to their bridegrooms/husbands and men are to love and cherish their wives as God loves the church. Men, you must understand that your wife is an extension of you. The Bible teaches that the body of Christ, which is the church, the bride of Christ, is an extension of Christ. Therefore it can be concluded that the woman/ bride/wife is an extension of her husband.

When you understand the stipulations that the Word of God has on the marital union, it makes you want to work harder at cooperating with one another to develop a happy, healthy, functional union. The one and only thing that helps one to remain focused on making marriage work and not treat it like a trial or a test is that God be in the marriage. This means putting God first in your life. This means accepting Christ as your personal Savior and allowing Him to rule and reign in every area of your life, including your marriage. This means making God the center of your union. Too many people take their vows lightly and that's one reason why statistics show that approximately 50 percent of marriages end in divorce. Some don't want to work on their relationship. Others feel like a marriage should not require work. Some feel that it's too much work.

Then there are those who think it's supposed to just be

bliss and happiness 24/7 like something out of the movies. You know, always in agreement, happy all the time, sensual, and sex all the time. This is unrealistic. In fact, if you observe the examples of the movies and television shows, you will see that they usually have multiple partners and/or marriages before the end of the show. One cannot base his or her relationship on Hollywood scenarios that are merely figments of a writer's imagination and fantasy that endures for a brief couple of hours. You cannot compare a few Hollywood scenes to a relationship God intended to last "unto death do us part." The secular appearance of a relationship is often not realistic or consistent with the reality of marriage. Reality reveals that 50 percent of marriages terminate. This is why it's vital to gain information and work on your marriage even if there are no apparent issues. There is always room for expansion and growth. Putting effort in a marriage will take it from happy to happier.

A perpetual blissful relationship would be everyone's optimal dream, but what happens when life and life's circumstances take precedence? What happens when the children come and their lives intermingle with the couple's? What happens when debt outweighs the income? What happens when disagreements make one or both of the individuals disagreeable? What happens when the time and energy for sex dwindles or disagreements hinder the sex? What happens when you're too stressed by life's circumstances to count your blessings and enjoy your mate? Yes, husband, you are to enjoy your wife; and wife, you are to enjoy your husband. You should enjoy every aspect of them. But what happens when life's circumstances take their toll on your relationship?

You must also understand that placing unrealistic

expectations on your marriage by going into the marriage with an unrealistic idealism of what a marriage should be is setting you up for failure from the start. As unique as every individual is the uniqueness of every marital bond. There are no two individuals who are exactly identical, even if they are identical twins. They two have different personalities. Each was uniquely designed by God. People are different. They have different desires. They have different needs. They like different things. They come from different backgrounds and bring different experiences to the mix. Despite some individuals' belief, marriage doesn't just turn out good but rather it takes work to make it good and to keep it that way. Don't formulate unrealistic expectations and place them on the union. Discuss with your mate what each of your expectations are for the union.

Another thing to know is that having expectations of someone else can lead to disappointment, frustration, heartbreak, and if not corrected, bitterness. You cannot expect something of someone that they did not promise. Men and women are fallible. We all make mistakes. Many make promises they don't intend on keeping or circumstances don't allow them to keep. If your expectations are too high, the majority of the time you will be let down. Don't place heavy unrealistic expectations on your partner. It may cause them to be weary of you. In other words, no one wants to consistently try to please someone who is never satisfied. If you are never satisfied, always "wanting" something, and never appreciative of what your mate does, you need to check yourself and your level of expectations. Don't allow this to make your mate insensitive to your needs because they just get tired of "all" your many expectations and become weary of trying to please you. Beware of and correct a selfish spirit. A selfish spirit is harmful to a union and if not corrected can be detrimental to a union.

Everyone has a propensity to be self-centered and self-willed, some more than others. Everyone has an innate desire to do what pleases them and it takes the grace of God for this to be rectified.

Romans 7:18–20 reads:

> For I know that in me (that is, in my flesh) nothing good dwells; for to will is present with me, but how to perform what is good I do not find. For the good that I will to do, I do not do; but the evil I will not to do, that I practice. Now if I do what I will not to do, it is no longer I who do it, but sin that dwells in me.

There is a constant struggle between the flesh and the spirit, a constant warfare between the flesh ruling or the dying of the flesh to the Word and will of God. It is important to yield to God so that flesh be crucified. This is vital not only for being a disciple of Christ but also for your marriage. If flesh is ruling in your marriage, it can be displayed as a selfish, self-centered person. Being self-willed can cause there to be unnecessary tension, heartache, and issues in your union that could be avoided if you would yield to the Lord and His principles. Being born again requires a dying of oneself and taking on the attributes of God and godly principles. Being in a harmonious blissful marital union requires a dying of one's selfishness (I, my, mine) and a taking on of what benefits the union (us, we, our).

Matthew 19:4–6 reads:

> And He answered and said to them, "Have you not read that He who made them at the beginning 'made

> them male and female,' and said, 'For this reason a
> man shall leave his father and mother and be joined
> to his wife, and the two shall become one flesh'? So
> then, they are no longer two but one flesh. Therefore
> what God has joined together, let not man separate."

In the sight of God, when a man takes a woman as his wife they become one. In the spirit and in the sight of God the husband and the wife are one flesh. Verse 5 reads, "and the two shall become one flesh." *Become* as defined in Webster's Dictionary means, "To pass from one state to another; to enter into some state or condition, by a change from another state or condition, or by assuming or receiving new properties or qualities, additional matter, or a new character." To become one literally means you exit or change from being in a single state to a married state. You change from two individuals into one union. You assume oneness. You adapt and take on what your mate likes. You take on his or her concerns. You adapt and take on new qualities and ways of doing things, going to different places and gaining new experiences. You're no longer your own man or woman but you are one. Your dreams must become entwined. Your goals must entwine. Your desires must become entwined. Your lives must entwine and become one.

Know that this is a process. It does not happen overnight. Everyone is unique. Everyone's embracement of the concept will be different. God's Word said, "and the two shall become one flesh," so in the sight of God it's done, but the manifestation timing is in the hands of the individuals. Just like all spiritual principles one must embrace and practice what God says, and this includes the marriage principles as well. One must practice being one with his or her mate so that "the two become one."

I cannot emphasize enough on the importance and value of praying and seeking the face of God regarding your mate that should have transpired prior to taking this life-changing step. This is one of the most significant steps that two people can make, and they should have received a release from God for their union prior to making their vows. If God gave a release for the union will it be perfect? No, humans are still fallible and there still will be issues, but with the help of God and the yielding of both mates God will be in the midst to make it easier and help you work through issues.

Second Corinthians 6:14 reads, "Do not be unequally yoked together with unbelievers. For what fellowship has righteousness with lawlessness? And what communion has light with darkness?" Being unequally yoked and not realizing it or ignoring it before your vows is a major problem! Here in this verse of Scripture Paul was making an appeal for the Corinthians to separate from unbelievers. If he was making it as a general appeal to believers, how much more is it pertinent for a couple intending to spend the rest of their lives together to be equally yoked?

Believers are to gain insight, example, and instructions from everything in the Bible. So here the term *yoked* was used. A yoke was made from wood they formed to fit the necks of oxen, horses, or whatever animal was being used to plow, work in a field or perform a deed, to connect them together. The yoke made it impossible for one to try and go right when the direction was to go left and the other one was obeying the command. If one was obeying the command and going left and the other was in defiance pulling right, it would bring stagnation and confusion. The yoke meant they had to work as a team, each pulling its share but both pulling the same load and accomplishing the desired goal.

When choosing the oxen, I believe several things were taken into consideration. They had to be of similar height to be yoked. They had to be around the same weight and build. They had to exhibit relatively the same strength. The yoke needs to be aligned so that both oxen are comfortable and the equipment is not tearing into the flesh of one, causing discomfort or injury.

When you are equally yoked with your mate, and it is vital that you be, one is not pulling the majority of the weight in any area, but it is equal. You both share similar and the same goals. You should both be on the same level or have similar levels of ambition so that you can successfully accomplish goals and dreams. You're both not only concerned about the union but actively conforming to the needs and structure of the union to make "us" work. You both are definitely to be born-again believers, and not just born-again but equally yoked born-again believers, meaning you're both on the same page spiritually.

Your devotion level to God should be the same or significantly similar. It's a struggle when one wants to give God more of them or "all of them" and the other just wants a "little dab a do me." It's a struggle when one wants to give God more of them or their all and the other is pulling back. When you are equally yoked, your union will be aligned so that both of you are comfortable and neither of you is experiencing discomfort or injury in any area because of one being misaligned. You must be "aligned" (mentally, physically, and spiritually), equally yoked and working together as a "team." It is beneficial when you both "pull" in the same direction, the right direction, directions ordained by God; this is what makes an effective team.

Keep in mind that because everyone is uniquely different, you can't expect your partner to know what you want, to know what pleases you, to respond to things the way you think he or she should, or to reciprocate affections the way you think he or she should. Some people for one reason or another are just unwilling to do certain things. Maybe because they are unfamiliar with them; maybe because they don't understand them; maybe because they don't know how; maybe because they just don't want to. But hopefully this book will open the readers' minds and hearts to change! In many instances some of you will have to totally shift your minds from preconceived ideas of what you believe marriage should be and what you think it entails. You may have viewed and admired someone else's marriage and are trying to replicate it…let it go. Understand that you just "viewed" as an outsider. You don't know what happened behind closed doors. You didn't experience the relationship up close and personal the way you are with your companion.

No relationship is perfect, because relationships are made up of imperfect, fallible people. People require a lot of work and some more than others. Say it out loud: "I require work!" Relationships require work. You may have images from your parents', a relative's, a friend's or acquaintance's marriage that you feel is a good example…let it go. Everyone is unique. Everyone's relationship is unique. You must learn to work to achieve what is best for the two of you. Both of you must work together to promote open communication so that you experience a loving relationship.

Matthew 7:12 reads, "Therefore, whatever you want men

to do to you, do also to them, for this is the Law and the Prophets." I believe if you make the "golden rule" your guide for your marriage it will help to keep things in the right perspective. Think about how you want your mate to treat you before treating him inconsiderately. Keep communication open and be clear without making your mate feel intimidated. Don't demand, but rather, communicate. Don't demean, but communicate. Don't be bossy, just communicate. Don't give ultimatums, choose to communicate. Marriage should be harmonious with romance. It should be loving, passionate, and fun! It is a union ordained by God and everything that God made is good!

TIPS

- Don't have unrealistic expectations for your mate

- Don't have unrealistic expectations for your union

- Make your marriage fun, loving, and happy

CHAPTER 1
ASSIGNMENT

1. Both of you write down at least five expectations you have of your marriage. Review them carefully and delete any unrealistic expectations before sharing the list with your mate.

2. Both of you openly discuss the list your mate shared with you. Don't get in a heated "discussion/argument." Discuss with an open mind.

3. List ways to implement them into your relationship.

4. Put a time frame on the implementation. Don't just say we can do it like this, but actually set the time for it to start and keep it.

Chapter 2

UNLOAD THE BAGGAGE

MARRIAGE IS A vow that was made before the Lord to your spouse. It is a covenant between two people. The fall of man and sin resulted in distortion, dysfunction, and fragmented individuals in every area of man's life. I believe that biblical truths parallel natural experiences and occurrences. The Old Testament taught that the spilling of blood bonded and consummated a covenant. In the Old Testament a sacrifice of a "pure" animal was made for the forgiveness of one's sins. In the New Testament it was the shedding of the blood of Jesus Christ as a perpetual remission of one's sins. When we accept Christ as our personal Savior, the shedding of His blood sealed the deal. It's a covenant that we are born again and saved from hell as long as we ask God for forgiveness of our sins and remain in right standing with Christ. It's a promise that we are the children of God and that He blesses those who remain in covenant with Him.

Even as blood was shed to bind a covenant in the Word of God, representing reconciling the people back in relationship with God, I believe it was the will of God that the "shedding" of blood was to seal the deal in the marital

15

union. It was to bind the covenant between husband and wife. The shedding of the female's blood, which occurs during the initial act of intercourse causing the tearing of the female's hymen by the penetration of the male, was to be the ultimate binding of the covenant between husband and wife. The ultimate and initial "becoming one" was to take place with one's life mate. The act of lovemaking causing the shedding of blood from the "pure" woman's hymen was to spill upon her husband's penis during penetration, consummating a blood covenant between husband and wife. It was to take place in the "marital bed" with one's mate. The woman being the receiver for the man's release binds them together. The exchanging of fluids during the sexual act forms an intimate connection. It's like he becomes a part of her and she becomes a part of him. The woman carries something of him and the man carries something of her. Both have invested of themselves physically and intimately in one another.

Even the world understood the importance of blood bonding. Back when I was a child, when friends wanted to prove their friendship was to be forever, they would show this by becoming a "blood sister or brother." This consisted of the pricking of a finger and a mingling of the blood together, which formed "the bond." That's not a good practice for today because of the many diseases that the blood can carry, but that's what was done "back then." Today they just say, "My BFF," meaning "Best Friend Forever." And like everything else of this generation, it has lost something. The commitment is not lasting. It's just words. The children and teens are BFFs with Mary in September but not hanging with her in January, and BFFs with Sue. I guess it's just a temporary arrangement like so many of the marriages that take place today. Back in the day divorce wasn't as prevalent as it is today. People tried to work it out and stick it out, but today some don't even work at it for a year before they terminate the relationship. It's a sign of the times…excuse my venting, it's just sad that commitment is being taken so lightly in the times that we're living in today.

The very act of lovemaking where two bodies become physically one, creating a oneness, was to be the very act that established a covenant bond between the man and the woman. It was to seal the deal for the marital covenant. One must understand that sin has afforded the "blood bonding" to occur, in many instances, with someone other than one's spouse. This is why so many individuals have "soul ties" with people who are not their mates. They've connected in a oneness that was intended for the married couple in a marital bed. They've formed a bond with someone other than their spouse. They've connected and exchanged acts of intimacy that should have only occurred with their spouse. This is why many individuals are carrying sexual baggage into their marriage, trying to compare their spouse with a past lover or lovers; trying to compare their marital sex with past sexual encounters. It is imperative to "let it go." It is baggage that can ruin a marriage if not released. God forgives us of past transgressions but we must also allow God to renew and cleanse our minds so that our past doesn't hinder our present and our future.

When one thinks about baggage it can be a number of things. Some perceive blended families as baggage. This deals with ex-spouses and/or children from previous relationships and all the baby's momma/baby's daddy drama that comes with it.

Soul ties from previous relationships can also be baggage. Prayerfully this was conquered prior to making the commitment with your spouse, but occasionally the commitment is made prior to soul ties being destroyed. Unresolved soul ties from a previous partner can affect your present relationship. Soul ties deal with the soul part of man, such as one's intellect; emotions; and the decision making process of one's will. "Soul ties" are as strong as the emotions and memories that were stored from the past experiences of a relationship.

Know that in order to make your present relationship be all that it can and should be, you must "clip" all former soul ties. Here are a few tips for this process: Remember the Bible says "old things are passed away behold all things become new." Stop reminiscing on fantasy. The mind has a way of making things appear more appealing than they actually were. Never compare your spouse with a past love or relationship. Embark on making new experiences, developing and experiencing new emotions, and making new memories with your spouse. And most importantly remember the old tie wasn't as good as your mind tries to make you think…if not death, something brought the relationship to an end.

Don't allow the enemy and your mind to keep you in bondage to the old when you can be free for the new. Let go of old baggage! Baggage can also include financial issues such as your partner being in a substantial amount of debt or making insufficient income. It can also be a partner with poor credit. This is especially an issue when the two of you try to make a large purchase like buying a house but continue to be turned down due to one of your credit scores. Baggage is also bad habits, addictive behaviors, or anything that brings negative ramifications on your relationship. Here, however, I'm going to be focusing on emotional baggage.

Genesis 1:31 reads, "Then God saw everything that He had made, and indeed it was very good. So the evening and the morning were the sixth day." Everything and everyone that God made was good, but the fall of man separated man from God. Therefore, confusion, pain, and sorrow, to name a few of the downfalls, along with everything else that sin entails, was added to the mix.

Man was created perfect and whole but disobedience and sin produced an imperfect fragmented being. Unfortunately, men and women are fragmented individuals and God wants to make us whole but we must be willing and yielded to God in every area of our lives to receive "wholeness." You cannot have areas of your personality, areas of your desires, areas of your thoughts, areas of your will that you don't allow God to deal with. You cannot selectively choose what you allow God to be a part of and what you choose to leave unsanctified and unchanged by God. When a person does this it leaves them fragmented, and this is why we see so many dysfunctional individuals. It is also why we see so many dysfunctional relationships.

People are broken and entering into relationships before allowing the Creator to deal with them, to heal them and make them whole. This produces relationships that are anything but whole, anything but complete, and anything but perfect. Many relationships are everything but happy and fulfilling. Many relationships don't last, but unfortunately those same individuals go into other relationships carrying the same mind-sets and problems into another relationship. This and the fact that hurts from prior relationships are transferred into a new relationship can terminate a relationship before it gets started. They carry the same unregenerate behaviors. They transfer the same thoughts. They utilize the same techniques for solving or not solving problems. Their same poor communication skills are transferred. And the same feeling that they're right and the other person is always at blame is carried into new relationships. What many fail to recognize is that the constant element in all of the relationships is "you." Every relationship that you're in…includes you.

Ephesians 4:22 reads, "That you put off, concerning your former conduct, the old man…" It's time for change. Change of mind. Change of heart. Change of reactions. Change of actions. Change of how to show love. As a believer you must "put off" the things of old. That means the way you conducted yourself before accepting Christ as your Savior must change. The way you conducted "old" past relationships must change and align with godly love and godly principles. The only common denominator in the new relationship is you.

Don't allow pride to hinder you from changing and maximizing a fun, loving, blissful relationship. Pride and stubbornness can hinder one's walk with God. It can hinder God's destiny for you. And it can also hinder a marital relationship. First Samuel 15:23 reads, "For rebellion is as the sin of witchcraft, And stubbornness is as iniquity and idolatry." Don't get it twisted. Staying stuck in your ways and refusing to change by saying "it's just me" or "that's the way my momma or daddy was" is not the right attitude. It's stubbornness, which is iniquity, which is sin.

There are several reasons for not changing. One: You don't want to. And to this I recommend you get a change of heart from God. Two: You don't know how to. To this I say follow the technique that you did to be a follower of Christ. You do what the Word of the Lord says and not what your flesh dictates. You give in to the Word of God and not your flesh. You just do the right thing in spite of what your emotions may be telling you to do. And lastly, you think it's too much work. And to this I say "get to working!" People tend to work on everything else but neglect their marriage. We work on our jobs/careers to do a good job so that we can get promotions. Some work on their physical appearance at the gym or some other regime to produce a healthy, sculptured physic. So why not put some energy and effort into a marital union? Your marriage may be experiencing issues now but you can make some adjustments and make it better. Your marriage may be OK now, but with a little more effort you can make it better. Your marriage maybe good now, but you can always make some adjustments and make it great.

So, you're with someone new; but if you refuse to change and grow you're still "you" carrying undesirable baggage into another relationship. What this produces is another relationship in that it's another party involved, but the same relationship in that the same dysfunctions follow the individuals. Unless an individual allows God to rid him of his baggage, he carries the baggage into other relationships. This compounds the situation by combining with the other individual's mind-sets and problems and it can ruin a marriage before it gets started. Everyone is a product of his or her past and present. In other words, you are you because of everyone and everything that has ever touched and/or influenced your life. Every good, every bad, every positive and every negative past interaction influences your reactions to present encounters. Every past relationship, whether good or bad, influences your responses to present and future encounters. This is why we must yield ourselves to God and allow Him to break negative cycles, traits, and attitudes in our lives so that we can progress and grow as opposed to remaining stuck and stagnant in behaviors, mind-sets and thoughts. God wants to deliver His people from their baggage (don't get offended or think you don't have baggage; everyone has some kind of baggage and some individuals more than others). He just needs a willing, yielded spirit to work with.

John 4:9–10 reads:

> Then the woman of Samaria said to Him, "How is it that You, being a Jew, ask a drink from me, a Samaritan woman?" For Jews have no dealings with Samaritans. Jesus answered and said to her, "If you knew the gift of God, and who it is who says to you, 'Give Me a drink,' you would have asked Him, and He would have given you living water."

God wants to give us living water; not stagnant water, but "water springing up into everlasting life." It's life changing. It's eternal life. It's the best life. It's freedom. In order to be freed from baggage one needs an "up close and personal encounter with Christ."

Verses 28–30 and 39 read:

> The woman then left her waterpot, went her way into the city, and said to the men, "Come, see a Man who told me all things that I ever did. Could this be the Christ?" Then they went out of the city and came to Him....And many of the Samaritans of that city believed in Him because of the word of the woman who testified, "He told me all that I ever did."

Notice that she spent some time with Christ. It was not a brief encounter, as it was a discourse that took place between them. One must spend some time in God's presence for Him to release them of unwanted baggage. One must experience an intimate encounter with God that frees one from their past and releases one for their present and future. It's an experience that's not only an inward subjective experience, but it flows outward and is objective for all to see. In other words not only will you know you've been freed, but others will know you've changed.

Procuring change and getting rid of baggage will take effort but it will be efforts well expended. To procure change a person must first admit and recognize that change is needed. As long as a person thinks everything is OK, change will not come. An individual must acknowledge that change is necessary.

Next the person must identify what change(s) are needed. Unless it is identified, a person's efforts will be aimless and unfocused. The problem area must be identified so that a targeted effort can be enforced. The first two points are relatively easy. All that's needed is for the individual to pray and ask God to "show me, me" and He will. No matter how many years you have been a believer, there's still some of "you" that needs to go. No matter what stage you are in with your relationship with Christ, there's still some of "you" that's lingering. No matter what your position is in the body of Christ, there's still some of "you" that you need to let go.

There is always room for growth and improvement. There's always another level that God is calling you to spiritually. As soon as you conquer and change in one area, there's another aspect that must be addressed. There are always higher heights and deeper depths in God. There are always new dimensions in God. There's always another level of intimacy in God, and changing and growing helps us to accomplish this.

The next step is to begin to implement change. Ask God to grace you to change and yield to the Word of God for implementation to be procured. It is a known, documented fact that when an individual wants to break a habit they should stop the habit and replace it with the new desirable habit. If this is done twenty-one consecutive days or times, then the new desirable habit should be in place and the undesirable habit eliminated. It's going to take discipline, but practice the new behavior and replace it where you used to exhibit the old behavior. Stop doing what you want and do what the Word of the Lord says. Stop doing things the old way and try something new. It's not going to happen overnight; be consistent and persistent. Practice perfects. It's a process, but you must desire to make it happen. The most important element is to keep it before God in prayer. Pray about change in you. Pray about personal change, spiritual change, and change in your relationship.

Remember it does not have to be a sin that you need deliverance from. It does not have to be a big problem. It just has to be baggage—anything hindering your relationship from going to the next level. Also remember your marriage may be fine, because many are, but you want to take it from OK to good, from good to better, from better to best. You want to go to the next level of bonding and intimacy with your mate. Just pray and seek the mind of God. There's always room for improvement in every area of one's life and relationship.

Many people are insecure because they have abandonment issues. Someone they loved and trusted in their past left them or let them down. Some individuals suspect that everyone cheats because they're a cheater or someone they loved cheated on them in a past relationship. Some are still carrying baggage from experiences incurred from childhood that is causing issues in their adulthood. You feel the way you do and react to things the way you do because of past experiences. You are you because of what has influenced you. Past experiences made you who you are now. What you are experiencing now is making up who you're going to be. People learn lessons from everything that touches their lives. Whether you realize it or not, you're learning something daily. Some learn what not to do by another's actions because they didn't like the outcome that the actions rendered. Some unfortunately follow the actions because they don't know how to implement change. The good thing is change can be implemented with the help of God and an open mind and willing spirit of an individual.

In order for your present relationship to blossom and grow you must let go of past baggage. Old wounds from past hurts must be released. If you were wounded by a previous partner, you cannot bring those fears, pain, disappointments, and suspicions into your present relationship. You cannot blame or punish your present partner for things that someone else put you through. It is imperative that you take your "baggage" to the Lord and leave it there. Your present relationship will not blossom and grow when you continue to hold on to old unresolved issues from past experiences and relationships. You must confront your issues personally and as a couple in order to freely love your mate and experience love at a deeper, more intimate level. You must give your new relationship with your spouse, who is your life partner, a new fresh start. You must learn to look at your mate with a fresh new outlook, not through the eyes of past hurts or experiences. Get rid of the baggage! I know this is easier said than done but you can do it with the help and strength of God.

Confronting issues is not easy, after all most people feel like they're wonderful and beautiful without faults and that "God loves me just the way I am." This is true. God does love you but God does want you to change. Change is good! Romans 6:6 reads, "Knowing this, that our old man was crucified with Him, that the body of sin might be done away with, that we should no longer be slaves of sin." One must drop off *all* the ways of the old man. If you used to harbor an argumentative spirit, you now have to learn to effectively communicate. You must learn and implement Proverbs 15:1: "A soft answer turns away wrath, But a harsh word stirs up anger." It is not wisdom to go "head to head" with your mate. It is wisdom to listen, get an understanding, and then respond to his or her concern. If your old man had anger issues the new man must stand on and operate on Proverbs 29:22, "An angry man stirs up strife, And a furious man abounds in transgression."

Ephesians 4:26–27 reads: "'Be angry, and do not sin': do not let the sun go down on your wrath, nor give place to the devil." It is crucial that one not allow their emotions and personality to cause them to ruin, in a couple of minutes, what a lifetime sometimes cannot rectify. You cannot be led by your emotions and allow them to ruin your relationship. I know that most of the time the women get blamed for this error, first with the monthly hormonal changes (PMS) and then with menopause. But I want you to know that some of you men are just as much like emotional roller coasters as some of the women…funny.

Never allow your temper, emotions, or anger to give the devil space to cause havoc in your relationship. If you struggle with "giving a piece of your mind" or getting in your point of view and you know that you say things out of your emotions and in anger, walk it out. When you feel this way, remove yourself from the situation. Put brief physical distance between you and your spouse. Go take a walk. Go into another room. Go pray. And to the mate:

Don't follow them; give them space to think and regroup. When you do have bouts of being angry (because you will), always come together and make it right before going to bed. I've seen couples go from being mad for a couple of hours to being mad and not talking for days. This is not good. Always get an understanding of the issue and come into an agreement with one another.

One thing is usually certain: because the two of you are different it usually means your emotional reactions are different. This means when one is "venting" on an issue the other's emotions are not normally on the same passionate level. So before the situation becomes escalated, the one who is calm should remain calm. Just let your mate vent. Don't say anything to escalate the situation. If you must reply (sometimes it may be better to hold your opinion until a later date), reply in wisdom. Two highly emotional individuals venting at the same time usually is not good because it escalates the situation. Another thing is a person usually knows ahead of time when something they desire to discuss may cause a problem. Wait until you have your emotions under control before bringing up the topic, and then do it in wisdom after putting prayer in the mix.

Spiritual as well as personal growth is important. Second Corinthians 5:17 reads, "Therefore, if anyone is in Christ, he is a new creation; old things have passed away; behold, all things have become new." Please know that if you ask God to reveal yourself to you, He will! Once He does, you must ask for grace to change. God can do it. You can do it. Everything that has life is constantly changing. Some change is involuntary such as the aging process. Other change is voluntary, such as is seen in the body of a body builder. As they work out and lift weights their body becomes visibly sculptured.

If your marital relationship is to grow and change for

the better, you must work on improving yourself and your union as faithfully as a body builder. But you must be willing to work on yourself and your relationship. If for some reason you're not hearing from God what areas you need to change, or you're not yielding to change on your own, it is advisable to find a good Christian counselor to assist you in navigating through your issues.

Matthew 7:12 reads, "Therefore, whatever you want men to do to you, do also to them, for this is the Law and the Prophets." Meditate on the "golden rule." Think about the way you treat your mate. Think about some of the behaviors that you're displaying. Do you want the same treatment? Would you tolerate some of the treatment that you are giving out? "Do unto your mate as you want them to do unto you."

TIPS

- Don't compare your mate to past partners.

- Don't hold on to old experiences expecting your mate to duplicate your past.

- Never voice comparison of an old partner to your mate.

- I don't believe it's wisdom to share explicit intimate details about a past lover/affair with your spouse. This will leave permanent images in his/her mind.

- Home is where you are free to be the "real" you. Make sure the "real" you is considerate and loving in spite of the day you've had or problems you're facing.

CHAPTER 2
ASSIGNMENT

1. Both of you examine yourselves. Pray and ask God to show you "baggage" you're carrying that you need to release.

2. Spend serious prayer time asking God to heal and change you. This will not happen overnight. It is a process. You must yield yourself to God and allow Him to bring change in you. You must also make every possible change that you can to line up with the Word of God and the dealings of God.

3. After identifying what you consider your baggage to be, ask each other what they perceive as your "baggage." Avoid being critical toward one another. Just state it cordially and lovingly.

4. List ways to implement correction.

5. List ways to unload the baggage and set a time frame to begin.

6. If necessary, schedule an appointment with a Christian counselor or spiritual leader/advisor.

Chapter 3

TWO ARE BETTER THAN ONE

Two are better than one, Because they have a good reward for their labor. For if they fall, one will lift up his companion. But woe to him who is alone when he falls, For he has no one to help him up. Again, if two lie down together, they will keep warm; But how can one be warm alone? Though one may be overpowered by another, two can withstand him. And a threefold cord is not quickly broken.

—ECCLESIASTES 4:9–12

THE WORD OF God says two are better than one. From the beginning God has demonstrated and conveyed the importance of unity with man and the unity of man with one another. In the beginning God created male and female that the male would not be alone. It is important that when you are married you realize there is no longer "I" and "me" but it is now "us" and "we." You are in a relationship and everything that you do must now benefit "us," not just "me." You must begin to have a different perspective on life in that you are now to assist in helping the union to succeed. You don't do what you may have done as a single when you're married. For example, you work but the money is no longer "my money" but "our money." Bills come first, not buying shoes, electronics, clothes, and so forth.

Be careful not to hurt your mate's feelings. You know you like to look at the opposite sex, but don't eyeball the candy to the point that it offends your mate. Pull yourself in! Don't do anything to devastate "us." Your dating days and more-than-one-person sexual days are over. You only date and sex your mate. I know this is Christian teaching and I shouldn't have to state this but I've been saved and in the church for more than thirty years and have been counseling over seventeen years. And I see and deal with individuals that have not grasped and adhered to sexual sanctification. Sexual indiscretions not only devastate a marriage, but they can terminate it as well! It's no longer "you" but "us." Don't do anything that's going to harm or devastate "us." Individuals grasp the concept of "us" at different degrees. Some never get it. Some partially understand it. But until you fully understand and operate at the "us" level your marriage will never reach its full potential.

Many times couples color coordinate their outward apparel to show an outward appearance of togetherness and unity. They go through the time and put the effort into an outward appearance, when many times their union is anything but togetherness and unity. Unity as defined by Webster's dictionary is "oneness of sentiment, affection or behavior." When there is unity there should be a oneness in spirit first, with God being the head, and then a oneness of spirit with one's mate. Both should be striving for oneness to benefit their union. Unity takes place inward first, which radiates outward. Unity begins within one's spirit from the core and radiates outward so that it should be exhibited in one's actions, behavior, reactions and communications.

Inward unity radiates in an unrestrained outward loving union that far exceeds coordinating apparel.

When God told Noah that He was going to send a flood upon the earth to destroy the ungodly, He instructed Noah to take ' two' of every creation into the ark. Genesis 7:9 reads, "Two by two they went into the ark to Noah, male and female, as God had commanded Noah." God wants His creations to get along; love one another; reproduce; take dominion; live harmonious and happily together the "two" of you as a couple.

Leviticus 26:8 reads, "Five of you shall chase a hundred, and a hundred of you shall put ten thousand to flight; your enemies shall fall by the sword before you." There is power in numbers. You should be able to accomplish more with the two of you working together as one than you can working alone. A marriage means you both are working toward the same goals and the same dreams. First and foremost, as Christian believers your union should be available to do the will of the Lord for you as a couple as well as personally. God has invested gifts in every believer. There is ministry in every believer. There is a plan of God for every believer.

There is a work for every believer to accomplish. Not everyone is called to pulpit or public ministry, but everyone is called to be a soul winner, and we all have kingdom purpose. Every individual is called to be a living example of a Christian. Everyone is called to "present your bodies a living sacrifice, holy, acceptable to God, which is your reasonable service" (Rom. 12:1). Everyone is called to fulfill his or her personal God-ordained destiny. God may have put your union together for the purpose of raising up a next generation prophet, pastor, missionary, or president from your union offspring. You have to be willing to obey God and be willing to yield to the plan of God for your union. Sometimes God puts individuals together for the purpose of fulfilling a kingdom purpose ministry team. Whatever the plan and purpose of God is, you must comply.

Understand that it is not the will of God that you try and compete with your mate. Your mate is to be viewed as an extension of you. He or she is a part of you. You are connected. Genesis 2:23 reads, "And Adam said: 'This is now bone of my bones And flesh of my flesh; She shall be called Woman, Because she was taken out of Man.'"

Competing against your mate is like competing against yourself. You must want to see one another succeed. You must want to see your partner's dreams fulfilled. You must want to see your partner's goals accomplished. Fulfilling goals builds self-esteem and gives a person a sense of self-worth. Accomplishing a dream or a goal makes your mate feel happy and good. If your mate is happy, you should be happy. If your mate is happy, your union is happy. You must want to see your partner look good. When he/she looks good, you look good. Whether naturally or spiritually, when he/she looks good it reflects you. The reflections of your mate reflects you. That's why some men get offended when their mate wants to dress too provocatively or vice versa. They don't want other men/women looking at what's theirs. It should be like that in every area. When your mate accomplishes something educational, you look good. When they get a promotion on their jobs or in the church, you should feel good and honored because he/she is an extension of you. Strive to complement one another, not compete against one another.

Matthew 18:19 reads, "Again I say to you that if two of you agree on earth concerning anything that they ask, it will be done for them by My Father in heaven." That in itself is powerful! Knowing that the two of you together just increased the damage you can do to the kingdom of darkness and the exploits you can do for the kingdom of God is powerful. When you work together, it is powerful. You broaden your horizons and expand your dimensions. With the two of you working together as "one" there is nothing that you can't accomplish in unity. Praying for the same issues…powerful! Praying for breakthrough together…powerful! Praying for financial issues as a team…powerful! Praying each other through…powerful! The enemy can't keep you down as long as you function as a team and operate in agreement.

You must also work together to accomplish and fulfill the goals and dreams that you have as a couple. Hopefully before you got married you shared your desires, dreams, and goals that you had for yourself personally and the ones you had for your union with your love. Hopefully your mate shared his or hers with you. And prayerfully they were similar and you both were in agreement for making them happen "together."

It is important for everyone to have goals for themselves. Having and striving to accomplish and fulfill goals gives a sense of self-worth. It boosts a person's self-esteem. There is nothing more rewarding than accomplishing something that was just a dream or a desired goal. To see your dreams become reality is awesome. The emotions are empowering to the fulfillment of additional goals and dreams. It makes you happy, and happy individuals make happier relationships. Make sure your goals as a couple collectively coincide. Your goals—personal/individual goals as well as the union's/couple's goals—should improve "us," not sever "us." In other words, if the goals are causing division in your relationship, they should be reevaluated and adjustments should probably be implemented.

Working together should be exemplified in every area of a marriage. There should be no "woman's work" or "man's work," but whatever it takes to get a job done. Believe me, it's not a problem to a woman if she comes home and her husband is cooking dinner. I don't believe it's a problem if the husband is cutting the grass and the wife pitches in and pulls up the weeds or does the trimming. It's all about working together so that one is not overloaded with duties and responsibilities while the other is laid back and fancy free. Discuss who will do which chores. Pitch in and work together. This is especially important in today's world where both spouses have jobs and are working outside of the home. Don't allow your mate to be exhausted with little or no free time while you have a lot of free time and can assist them and alleviate their load.

So now that you're married this is the time to unite together and make each other's personal as well as the union's "us" goals happen. This is the time to work together and fulfill dreams, fulfill goals, reach accomplishments, and make memories. Don't renig on your promises to one another but strive to fulfill those promises and make one another happy. Matthew 12:25 reads, "But Jesus knew their thoughts, and said them: 'Every kingdom divided against itself is brought to desolation, and every city or house divided against itself will not stand.'" Work together as a team and allow Matthew 7:12 to be your guide: "Therefore, whatever you want men to do to you, do also to them, for this is the Law and the Prophets."

Tips:

- Don't allow anyone to bring division in your relationship.

- Never respect another man or woman's opinion over your spouse's.

- Don't run your mate down to someone else.

Chapter 3
Assignment

1. Each of you share two short-term personal goals with your mate (something you want to happen within the next six to twelve months).

2. Each of you share two short-term goals for "us" with your mate (something you want to happen within the next six to twelve months).

3. Each of you share two long-term personal goals with your mate (something you want to happen in the next four to five years).

4. Each of you share two long-term "us" goals with your mate (something you want to happen in the next four to five years).

5. Write out ways to prepare for all the goals. Set a time frame for implementation and start working toward it.

Take time and use effective communication skills. Look at your partner when talking. Don't put down their ideals and aspirations.

Chapter 4

CAPITALIZE ON THE DIFFERENCES

THERE IS A saying that "opposites attract," which proves to be true in most marriages. People are attracted to people who are different than themselves. Humans are intrigued by difference. In science the positive ion attracts the negative ion. And so it is with people; we're usually attracted to what we don't have or what's different to us.

Individuality is what makes you unique. In marriage you have things in common with your mate, but then a lot of things are different and sometimes completely opposite. This is noted many times by the one mate liking a warmer temperature in the home while the other likes it a little cooler. One may be a spender while the other is a saver. One may be a morning person and the other is not. Differences can also be in romance. One person is romantic and the partner is not. God in His infinite wisdom and diversity made everyone uniquely and specifically one of a kind. We are all important and special to God. We were placed on earth to be used by God and to live in harmony with one another, especially in marriage and in the body of Christ. We are made to complement one another, and it is our job to learn how to capitalize on and work our differences to maximize the strength of our marital union, to birth our potential and fulfill divine purpose.

You must realize that everyone is a unique individual. You and your spouse grew up differently. Some people grew up with two parents in the home while others grew up in a single-parent home. Your spouse may be used to having a male figure in the home but you did not grow up with this experience. No two individuals have the same exact experiences even if they appear similar to the objective eye. Some of them may be similar but never exactly the same; that's what makes you, you. Some individuals are good with numbers and budgeting; some are a little challenged in this area. One may be a virgin to marriage while the other may have been married before.

Don't allow your differences to put you at odds with one another but rather capitalize on them. Use your differences as an opportunity to learn new things from each other. Use them as an avenue to experience new things. Learn to do positive things that you might not have done if you hadn't met your mate. Be open to new experiences. Be open to going to different places. Maybe your mate has experienced cultural activities but you have not. Instead of rejecting the opportunity and blocking the experience because it is different and new to you, which may make you feel or view it as "strange," be open. Try going to a play because your partner wants to. So you like seafood, mix it up and try Italian if that's what your mate likes. Experience a sports event because your partner wants to. Many times you will find that you too can and will "grow" to like it.

Humans are precarious creatures. Sometimes they reject what's unfamiliar without giving it a chance. How can you say you don't like what you've never tried? Learn and experience positive new things from your mate. The diversity will keep your relationship alive and growing. Trying and experiencing new things will help keep your relationship from becoming stagnant and boring. It will keep it blooming and growing. It will make it interesting and exciting. Diversity in a relationship lowers the risk of the marriage becoming routine. Understand that too much routine can produce boredom for most people. Boredom can be an opening for the enemy to enter and produce havoc in your marriage. It is important that you know your mate. Some individuals get bored faster than others. Being flexible and versatile will allow diversity in the relationship to flow. Be open to experimenting and trying different things. Try going to different places, making memories and gaining new experiences.

Don't allow your differences to cause division. Don't argue because of difference but use it as an opportunity to learn and grow. Realize that you are both unique individuals and that this will cause disagreements from time to time, but learn to disagree without being disagreeable. Don't "make a mountain out of a mole hill." Agree to disagree without demeaning or hurting your love's feelings. You can disagree but still not say or do hurtful harmful things to one another. Don't allow a little disagreement to turn into a full-blown argument that lasts for hours, which can turn into days of disagreeing and hardly speaking. "It's not that serious!" Time is much too short for that. Have fun with one another.

You and your spouse's differences can actually bind your relationship closer together. Sometimes what the one doesn't possess the other does. This can be good for the union. This can help the union to succeed. For example, if one is a saver and good with numbers, this can be an asset. Allow this person to pay the bills and do the house budget while you just look over the books and come into agreement, and be in agreement. Just think about it: How much can you accomplish with the spender having the checkbook? You will accomplish more with the thrifty person doing the books. You can make a budget plan together for vacations, trips, cars, a house, and so forth.

In the body of Christ there are countless unique gifts but they all are supposed to work together so that the church can fulfill kingdom purpose. All gifts are needed. All talents are needed. Everyone is to bring his or her unique personality and self to the "body" to fulfill one "purpose," which is kingdom purpose. So it is in a marriage; both individuals are to bring their gifts, their talents, their resources, their knowledge, their finances, their opinions, and their experiences to the relationship to maximize the potential of the marital union. Both partners are to allow their differences to benefit the union, not sever it. Differences can give the union a better dimension. Don't shut down something because it is unfamiliar or new to you. Allow your differences to be a spice of life. Capitalize on the differences and mix it up!

TIPS:

- Don't reject and say you don't like something you never tried.

- Don't be judgmental or critical of your mate's differences.

- Maximize your union by capitalizing on your differences.

CHAPTER 4
ASSIGNMENT

1. Each of you write down at least three differences between you and your mate.

2. Write down how it affects your union.

3. Give thought to how the differences can complement your union.

4. Share your information with one another.

5. Each of you write down at least two new things you would like to do.

6. Share them with your mate.

7. Make plans to try them and follow through.

Chapter 5

COMMUNICATE

COMMUNICATION IS AN intricate part of the marital union. Communication is the key to every relationship, whether a business or personal relationship. It is important for one to effectively function in the activities of daily living. You must know how to communicate at some level to shop in stores. Communication is merely the act of the interchanging of knowledge. To be an effective communicator one must be able to convey and interchange one's thoughts or opinions to another in a way that the other person will be able to understand. If you are talking and the person you are talking to does not understand what you're saying, you are not being effective and your communication is invalid.

When you look at people in the business world you will see how the persons with good communication skills are usually the ones who get promoted. The person who exhibits exceptional public relations skills is usually the one that climbs the ladder of opportunity at a faster rate. In a marital relationship it is the couple that knows how to effectively communicate with each other that is happier. They work together more effectively. They meet their goals and dreams together. They accomplish things together and their relationship is usually more fulfilling. They respect one another and they're not yelling and trying to get their point across, but they're listening and communicating appropriately.

Usually there are different types of individuals that formulate unions. Some people are outgoing while others are reserved. There's usually one that likes to talk and then there's one that does more listening. If this does exist in your union, be sure to give space and opportunity for the "listener" to voice his or her opinion; you may discover that they have excellent input but are just a little reserved about sharing. Unfortunately, if two talkers are in a union this can be difficult if no one wants to listen to the other person's ideas, needs, opinion, and so forth. In order to show respect you must be willing to listen to the other person's point of view.

It can also be just as difficult if both parties are reserved, preferring to listen as opposed to expressing their opinion. This can work for a minute but eventually someone will become tired of always holding in his or her opinions. You must work to make sure the relationship is not "one-sided," where one person—the same person—is always voicing his or her opinions while the other person never gets his/ her opinions heard. Make sure one person is not always getting their needs met while the other is not. Make sure one person is not always getting things the way they want and the other person is unsatisfied, yet quiet. This dissatisfaction can become fatal to your marriage!

In order to be a good communicator you must be a good listener. Have you ever been in a conversation with someone but it was like two separate conversations taking place? It was like you were talking about the cars but the other person was discussing the weather. He or she was talking about one topic while you talked about a totally different topic. Or worst yet, you were both talking about the same topic but neither of you was listening to the other person enough to make a connection, you were both just voicing your viewpoints. Whenever your mate is talking to you (especially about something important or that they feel is important), you need to be listening, not construing and organizing your thoughts for a "comeback" answer or putting your thoughts together to take the conversation where you want it to go. When you do this it shows disinterest in their opinions and ideas; it shows disrespect to your partner; it shows selfishness; it shows you're not *listening*. It is good to be with "one accord" and in sync with your partner in conversation. You'd be surprised how many disagreements, arguments, misinterpretations, and misunderstandings could be avoided, if you'd just listen and participate in "the same conversation."

Another thing to keep in mind is that it is not always necessary for you to voice your viewpoint about everything. If you're not careful, expressing your viewpoint can come off as judgmental. This will make your partner clam up and hold things in, if they feel like you're judging their viewpoint in a criticizing manner. Allow him or her to express themselves without you being so opinionated. And when you do speak let it be in a courteous, caring, and loving manner.

Remember, effective communication is not all about talking. Effective communication includes effective listening. You must be a good listener in order to be a good communicator. When someone, your mate, is talking, you should not be trying to put together what you want to say, or thinking about what you want or need; thinking about how you feel; or trying to figure out how to interject your point of view…you should be listening. Pay attention and be empathic, especially if the topic is important to your mate. Try putting yourself in their shoes. How would you feel if you were trying to share something that's important to you and they weren't being attentive to you? Let him or her know you're listening by your attentive posture and the fact that you're able to respond without them having to repeat themselves.

Pick the right time to communicate. Try not to communicate if your mate is involved in another activity that he or she enjoys. Example #1: Your man has been waiting to watch the game all week. The game is finally on and you decide to talk. You had many opportunities all week to talk but you pick his time to watch the game to talk just to see if he'll listen. This is not right. Pick a more convenient time for both of you. Example #2: Your wife told you she was going shopping with her girlfriends on Saturday. You decide right before she's ready to leave on Saturday that you want to talk. This is not right. Pick a convenient time for both of you and choose an atmosphere that is conducive for communicating. Choose a time and place where there will be no distractions, giving each of you time to converse effectively.

Allow both individuals to play a part in the relationship. Allow both parties to express themselves. Understand that nagging is not communicating. Nagging is merely complaining, and most of the time criticizing. In order to effectively communicate one must be able to express him or herself in a cordial manner. Not yelling. Not criticizing. Not with attitude. Not venting in anger. Not using hurtful words. But relaying your feelings and expressing your concerns, wants, and needs in a respectful, loving manner to your "love," your life mate. I've found that when couples hold things in for a period of time they can begin to hold grudges and become frustrated, which makes their way of communicating come across as criticizing, demanding, and demeaning.

Instead of allowing things to get to this point, address issues sooner than later. Don't let issues mount up. It is more effective if you wait for the proper opportunity, when both parties are being cordial, and then state your position without being argumentative. I've found a good way to do this is to not put your mate down but rather state how you feel. Here are a couple examples to assist you in this process.

Instead of saying this:

> You're just lazy and think I'm your maid. You drop your socks and underwear on the floor like I feel like cleaning up after you. I've got better things to do. And why can't you even take out the trash? You need to do something around here!

Try saying this:

> It would really be helpful to me if you'd put your socks and underwear in the hamper. Also, could you take the trash out? When you help me around the house, it makes me feel like we're a team and it gives me time and energy to do other things.

Side note: If your partner has more energy because you're helping out it may benefit you later!

Instead of saying this:

> We didn't get this bed just for you to sleep in it. You haven't given me sex in awhile and I'm sick of this. I didn't get married just to sleep next to you!

Try this:

> You make me feel desirable and loved when you make love to me. Come on over here and let me hold/love you.

> You catch more flies with honey than you do with vinegar.

Honestly, most of the time it is the woman that does the "nagging"; but then there are a number of men that have the "nagging" tendency as well. If you're one who tends to nag, stop it! Be informed, people don't like being nagged. It is not a desirable trait to exhibit.

Why is it usually the woman who does the majority of the nagging? Women have a tendency to hold things in for a minute, which allows things to mount up. They take things for a long time, which unfortunately allows feelings and emotions to come to a head. Then they just need one thing to push them over. It doesn't have to be serious. It doesn't have to be important. It doesn't even have to be the problem at hand. It's just the "needle that breaks the camel's back," and then you put your woman on a roll of complaints, criticizing…nagging.

Now I'm not going to leave you men out. Usually the woman has given you some type of "clue." She's been telling you subtly, and in some cases directly, but some men have a way of not listening, possibly ignoring or simply just not getting it. And to give some of the men credit, some women have a way of talking while the husband is pre-occupied, which means he's not fully paying attention and probably not listening. Don't try and talk while he's watching TV and think he's listening.

This brings up two points. First: Women, men don't communicate like you. Give them their space and know that even when they do communicate most of the time they will not share their emotions like you. Does that mean he doesn't care about you? Does that mean he doesn't love you? Probably not; it just means men and women are wired differently. Come right out and sweetly tell him what you're saying. Leave no room for him to guess what you mean. Say what you mean. They are not mind readers any more than you are, so this goes both ways. Both of you say what you mean; don't leave room for guessing and misunderstandings. Second, listen attentively to one another and address both parties' concerns. Men, listen to your wife. Look attentively into her eyes when she speaks and *listen*.

When you disagree about something, disagree without being disagreeable, with the end result bringing an agreeable solution. Come to a solution that the two of you agree on and can live with. You don't have to treat your spouse as the enemy because you aren't seeing eye to eye on a topic. They are still your friend; your lover; your partner; the one you choose to marry and be with "until death do us part." There will be countless times when you have a difference of opinion, but you must still keep communication open and effective. Neither party benefits if one shuts down and refuses to listen or participate in "sharing." Disagreements should not turn into out-of-control arguments.

An important element to remember is that whatever concerns your partner concerns you. Whatever his or her need is should become your need. Regardless of how you may feel about what they are sharing, if it concerns your mate, it is valid and it must be addressed. To dismiss his or her concerns as childish, dumb, stupid, unimportant, insignificant, etc. will only build a wall between the two of you, which, if left unresolved can cause your marriage to become stagnant or terminate.

If you loved your spouse enough to want to spend the rest of your life with them, you must love them enough to validate their emotions, feelings, needs, desires, concerns, and ideas; and enough to listen and address them so that implementation can take place to rectify their concerns. *Concern* as defined in the Webster's Dictionary means, "to relate or belong to, in an emphatical manner; to affect the interest of; to be of importance to."

Concerns are personal. They are subjective but they are also valid to the person who expresses them. Regardless of how you may feel about your spouse's concerns, you must not dismiss them as trivial. Again, if it is a concern to your partner, it is a concern to you! Don't dismiss it without giving it serious thought, deliberation, and some implementation. Don't dismiss it without giving your partner space to express their feelings. Don't dismiss it without discussing and implementing change to rectify the concern. One person's thoughts, ways, emotions, concerns, feelings, needs, and ideas are not the *only* priority. The two shall become one...your mate's concerns are as important as yours.

A marriage involves two personalities coming together to become and be one. So listen to your partner. Listen attentively. Acknowledge his or her concerns and repeat what he or she is saying in your own words. This shows you're listening and getting an understanding. This will also reduce the chance for misinterpretations and eliminate a lot of misunderstandings. Listen openly. Listen and get an understanding of how they feel and then work on a mutual solution. Good communication is all about good negotiating skills. It is a give-and-take, not a one-sided directive relationship. Yes, the man is the head, but he must work with his "helpmate," not dictate.

There will be times when the two of you disagree; but be agreeable. Continue to respect your mate in spite of the disagreeable topic. You can express yourself, but do it respectfully and lovingly. Voice it but don't wear it out. Say it and let it go. Try to be peaceable, remaining cool-tempered even if you're dealing with a "hot" topic. Your partner has a right to his or her opinion. You partner has a right to his or her feelings. Your partner has a right to his or her desires. What your partner doesn't have a right to is being insensitive and not respectful enough to allow the other mate to voice their opinions, needs, desires, ideas, feelings, and so forth. In order for communication to be effective you must learn to listen without cutting your partner off. No one likes to be dismissed without being heard. No one likes being interrupted without attention being given to his or her viewpoint.

Husbands, understand that women talk to connect with you, so be loving and understanding. Sometimes they just want to know you're listening. Sometimes they just want your attention. They don't necessarily want you to try and fix anything; just lovingly give your wife your undivided attention while she shares and communicates with you. Men, understand that women often talk to share with you and vent to you. Women, understand that when you vent to your man it's in his nature to fix. When a man loves a woman he tries to fix the "broken" problem or issue for her because he wants to make her happy; it's what men do. Women vent, and talking out loud it helps them to come to a solution; she talks it through. Men, on the other hand, hear what their woman is saying and try to fix it for her. Women, if you don't want him to fix it, don't make it appear to be broken and in need of fixing.

Wives, be considerate of the times you choose to share. Don't choose to do it while he's watching a game he's been waiting to see all week to determine if he cares more about you than the game. Women, understand that men try to "fix" things. They don't necessarily communicate to connect with you; they have other ways of connecting with you.

Wives, also understand that most men don't want to deal with a lot of "mushy" emotional stuff all the time. Also, keep the drama out of the union. No one wants to deal with constant drama in their life or marriage, so leave that entertainment for the movies. Men tend to feel that their being there with you is connecting. On a side note, women don't feel connected if you're in one room relaxing, on the computer, watching TV, or involved in another activity while she's in another room doing something else the majority of the time. It's great and it's important to have private time but don't just spend the majority of your home time in separate rooms. Spend time doing things together and maximize quality time. It's not in the quantity as much as the quality!

It is also important to understand that good communications is not blame passing. Don't waste time trying to prove it's your mate's fault, and that you're not the one to blame. It is better to avoid statements such as, "If you hadn't done ______ then we wouldn't be in this situation." Things are better handled when the problem is addressed without addressing your mate as the problem. Address the underlying problem. What caused the problem? Was it because of a misunderstanding? If so, work on that. Was it because your mate doesn't want to submit? If so, work on that. Was it because of a behavior that keeps recurring, causing the same or similar situation to manifest? If so, work on eliminating that behavior. Instead of focusing on who caused what, focus on a resolution to the problem and deal with and solve one problem at a time.

Think before you speak. You can't take it back once it's put out there! Sometimes we all give answers or opinions without processing the thought. This can sometimes be unwise. Always think about what you say and the attitude you say it in, or you may regret it later. If you put it into the atmosphere, it's there for good. You can't retract it or the damage that it caused down the line.

Also, you don't have to voice everything you feel. Feelings are emotions that are governed by a person's present state of mind. Some emerge from stress, some from hormones, some from anger, and so forth. Don't allow your present state of mind to cause you to release your present feelings and emotions into verbal expressions that don't align with your core feelings. In other words, don't say something now that you really don't mean because of what you're experiencing or feeling at the present time. It can't be retracted. Ephesians 4:29 reads, "Let no corrupt word [communication] proceed out of your mouth, but what is good for necessary edification, that it may impart grace to the hearers." Don't allow your emotions or your partner's actions and reactions make you respond and react inappropriately. You cannot control someone else's behavior, but you can control your own actions and reactions in every given situation.

Know that honesty is always important. *Honesty* in

Webster's Dictionary means, "frank sincerity; in principle, an upright disposition; moral rectitude of heart." Being honest means being fair when dealing with someone. *Rectitude* is defined in Webster's Dictionary as, "rectitude of mind is the disposition to act in conformity to any known standard of right, truth or justice."

The world has taught men and women to play games with one another. The sexes have learned to play games to attract the opposite sex; play games to keep their attention; play games with someone's emotions; play games with someone's heart; which, in essence, is playing with someone's life. Men are taught and encouraged to be "players," and women are taught and encouraged to be "divas."

When you get married, it is not to play games with someone's feelings, heart, or life; but it is to be in a loving, committed relationship that was designed to last "until death do you part." Don't get it twisted; I'm not saying that you should not play with your mate and have fun with your mate, because you should in that aspect. I'm saying, don't play with his or her feelings, heart, and emotions to benefit yourself, which causes them hurt and pain. The relationship cannot grow and possibly will not last if someone is into playing games and not being honest with their mate. Understand that true rectitude belongs only to our God; but if you are a born-again believer, you are to emulate your heavenly Father in love, truth, and honesty.

Romans 12:2 reads, "And do not be conformed to this world, but be transformed by the renewing of your mind, that you may prove what is that good and acceptable and perfect will of God." You must change what you learned about what a marital relationship is supposed to be like in the world and align your mind, align your thinking, align your thoughts, and align your processing of emotions with the Word of God! It doesn't matter what society says. What does the Word of the Lord say? It doesn't matter what your friends say. What does the Word of God say? It's not important what you've "always" done in the past in relationships. What does the Word of God say? Side note: If what you did in the past in other relationships was so profound, why are you in another relationship now? Why didn't that relationship last? Apparently your old "stuff" didn't work; so try some new "stuff." Try the Word of God and change your old pattern.

I realize that being honest means being vulnerable, and being vulnerable means you're opening up yourself to the possibility of someone being able to wound you or break your heart; but being "open" is a crucial part of the marital relationship. That's why it's so important to pray about whom you marry before you marry. You must be able to open up and share with one another in total honesty; open up in communicating; open up about finances, who's responsible for what, what the union's financial goals are; open up about sexual needs and desires, what works for you and what doesn't, what satisfies you and what doesn't.

To be vulnerable means that you must trust someone else with your feelings knowing that there is a possibility that you may be hurt. Humans are fallible and we do make errors from time to time. The good thing is, the more someone loves God and obeys God, yields to God and allows God to bring change in them, the less likely that their fallibility and errors will devastate you or the relationship. One's love for God will keep them in line. One's desire to please God will keep them in line. This is why it is vital to the marital union for the couple to be equally yoked and make God the center of their union. Trust depicts the relationship's demeanor. If you decide to be dishonest, understand it is never a "one time" lie but that it is ongoing. Most lies have to be continually covered by other lies to keep the initial lie from being exposed. This takes too much work! Practicing honesty is not only easier but it's also the right thing to do. It will bind the relationship together and enforce the bond.

Effective communication is the key to a successful, happy marriage. Communication is the bridge that negotiates agreeable financial strategies, submission, and sexual pleasure/fulfillment. Effective communication helps couples to capitalize on their differences and grow closer together as one. Therefore, couples should learn to communicate with one another without being judgmental and critical of the other's opinions. Learn to communicate patiently with your mate in a non-confrontational manner. Understand that no one wants to be talked to in a demeaning manner. You are both adults and deserve respect as adults. You both bring something to the table.

Another thing to remember is timing. Timing is important. Don't try to bring up additional conflicting issues when the one at hand is eruptive; this will only escalate the situation. Deal with and handle the pressing issue before going to the next one. Handle one issue at a time. Try to avoid bringing up past issues and the way your mate reacted or acted; how they handled or didn't handle something; or what they said or did in the past. If at all possible, leave the past in the past and deal with the present unless the present issue is a product of the past.

Try to discuss every problem or situation in a non-threatening atmosphere and manner. Don't wait too long to discuss issues. Waiting for prolonged periods to discuss issues allows things to fester, which can cause your relationship to deteriorate. Attack the problem, not the person. When you have to address issues that may offend your mate, always be tactful. Don't criticize; just state your opinion and always interject compliments. In other words, find a positive trait your mate has in spite of the issue and compliment along with your concerns about the present issue, which is going against the grain. This way it will not be perceived as being totally critical. You will find that your partner will be more open and receptive to you, and it will promote them to make adjustments and changes to improve the situation.

Look at your spouse when they are talking. Practice good listening skills. That means don't be thinking about what you want to say and how you can interject your thoughts. This causes confusion. This causes unnecessary conflicts because you "thought" he or she said something or meant something that they didn't say or mean because you weren't really listening. You instead were concentrating on what you wanted to say and how you could interject it. Honesty is the best policy, but do this lovingly; not with hurtful intentions, but rather to open up communication to take your union to a deeper level of intimate communing and loving experience.

Proverbs 18:21 reads, "Death and life are in the power of the tongue..." Avoid assassination of your mate with words. It is not wisdom to allow your tongue to hurt your spouse with words and kill your relationship. Remember, good effective communication is the key to a great relationship—it is the glue that holds it all together! Learn to use positive tactics as opposed to negative tactics.

It is better to give compliments that exalt your spouse than demeaning comments, which tear down their self-esteem. Build one another up in love. Everyone likes receiving compliments. Some individuals don't know how to receive compliments; if this is your mate, give them to him or her anyway. Compliment one another daily. It feels good to hear your spouse say things like, "you look good"; "that was a delicious meal you fixed"; "that outfit hugs you just right"; "you make me feel good"; "I appreciate/love the way you take care of the house"; "I appreciate you"; "I love the way you love me;" and so forth. Compliments makes a person feel desired, appreciated, and loved. It will let them know you don't take them for granted. Never shut communication down in your marriage regardless of the circumstance. Being silent usually means someone is hurt or angry. It can also mean indifference, meaning that an individual is unconcerned about the issue and/or the person presenting the issue enough to voice or have an opinion. Keep communication open. Don't shut down and allow things to build up; this can hinder every area of a marriage.

In Genesis chapter 11, there is an example of what people can do when they communicate and are on the same page:

> Now the whole earth had one language and one speech. And it came to pass, as they journeyed from the east, that they found a plain in the land of Shinar, and they dwelt there. Then they said to one another, "Come, let us make bricks and bake them thoroughly." They had brick for stone, and they had asphalt for mortar. And they said, "Come, let us build ourselves a city, and a tower whose top is in the heavens; let us make a name for ourselves, lest we be scattered abroad over the face of the whole earth." But the LORD came down to see the city and the tower which the sons of men had built. And the LORD said, "Indeed the people are one and they all have one language, and this is what they

begin to do; now nothing that they propose to do will be withheld from them. Come, let Us go down and there confuse their language, that they may not understand one another's speech." So the LORD scattered them abroad from there over the face of all the earth, and they ceased building the city. Therefore its name is called Babel, because there the LORD confused the language of all the earth; and from there the LORD scattered them abroad over the face of all the earth.

—GENESIS 11:1–9

Now here the people were walking in rebellion and pride building a city and a tower that would touch the heavens. Therefore, their efforts of the construction brought judgment; but let's look at the positive side. Their communication was effective enough to get the job done. The Lord said in verse 6, "Now nothing that they propose to do will be withheld from them." If you and your mate can effectively communicate, you will have a successful, blissful, happy, prosperous, healthy marriage. "Nothing that the two of you purpose to do will be withheld from you." The devil knows this; that is why he tries to intercept and not allow couples to communicate cordially and effectively with one another.

Communication is the key to success in every area of your marriage. Matthew 7:12 reads, "Therefore, whatever you want men to do to you, do also to them, for this is the Law and the Prophets." Think before you speak. Talk to your mate the way you want them to talk to you. Avoid being short and snapping at him or her, even when you're stressed. When there is effective communication there is nothing that the two of you can't accomplish together. Talk. Talk. Talk. Talking and listening to one another—effectively communicating will keep the two of you connected. Communicating is what will take your relationship from the ordinary everyday married couple to the extraordinary happily married couple.

Tips:

- Take time to think before you speak.

- Good effective communication is the key to success for a healthy, loving, fulfilling relationship.

- Look at your mate when communicating. Be considerate of his or her feelings. Lovingly understand even if you don't agree.

- *Listen!* Don't be thinking about what you want to say… *listen.*

- Appropriate timing and good negotiating are important factors for good communication.

- It takes two to argue.

- Once you put it out there, you can't take it back.

CHAPTER 5
ASSIGNMENT

1. Each of you write down three things you've wanted to discuss with your mate but haven't yet.

2. Cautiously put them into effective communication form.

3. Each of you discuss your list with your mate. Both of you utilize effective communicating skills. Be a good listener. Be courteous.

4. Each of you list at least three compliments about your mate.

5. Share your list with each other.

Chapter 6

SUBMISSION

S UBMISSION IS A general spiritual principle that applies to every area of an effective Christian's walk with God, including marriage. The fifth chapter of Ephesians deals with how an individual filled with the Spirit is to live in order to be an effective Spirit-filled believer. They are to receive repeated fillings and renewing of the Spirit thus taking on some of Christ's attributes and allowing God to be in control of their lives.

First let's begin with the golden rule found in Matthew 7:12 which reads, "Therefore, whatever you want men to do to you, do also to them, for this is the Law and the Prophets."

Ephesians 5:21 reads, "Submitting to one another in the fear of God." According to the dictionary, *submit* means "to surrender; to yield one's person to the power of another; to give up resistance." When you submit to one another in marriage it is not as in a hostage situation to the enemy but as unto the one you love. As unto the one *you* chose to marry. You submit without resisting, without arguing or causing a big blown out of proportion argument, and without grumbling and complaining.

Submission does not come easy for most individuals because most struggle to give up their independence. Everyone has his or her own agenda, own needs, own wants; but submission is crucial for natural as well as spiritual growth. You can't maintain a job without submitting to your employer and supervisors. You can't grow spiritually until you learn and practice submitting to God and the leadership He has placed you under. Your marriage won't blossom and grow until you learn to submit to one another. You're no longer two but one, and your partner's needs, desires, wants, goals, dreams, feelings, and emotions are as important as your own. It is your job as their mate to assist in their fulfillment.

Submission is important in a Christian family and it should all operate out of the spirit of love for one another. Love should cause submission. The more a person feels loved, the more they want to please the one who's showing the love. The more you love someone, the more you want to give or do for that person. "What I do for you is because I love you and it's the right thing to do." Understand that it is the will of God that His people submit to Him. He does not force us to submit. God does not force His children to submit to Him but rather we are to submit because it is His will; we love Him, and we want to please Him. So it is in the marital relationship; one partner is not to try and force the other to submit. Not physically (keep your hands to yourself unless it's for loving). Not verbally. Not with emotional manipulation (I'll leave if you don't do____). Love them into submission. Love should cause submission, not fear. A little side note: submission is a result of trust and love. The more you love and trust your mate, the easier it is to yield without resisting.

Don't get it twisted; submission and controlling are

different. One should never try to control their mate. To control, according to Webster's Dictionary, means "to overpower; to subject to authority; to restrain; to have superior force, or authority over." One should not control their spouse. One should not strive to "keep him or her in check." If you or someone you know are operating at this level, the person who's submitting is submitting out of fear, and you or the person exhibiting the behavior to control is operating out of his or her own inadequacies and inferiorities. This is definite baggage that needs to be released so that healing can manifest. Remember, submission should always be guided by love, never force. This includes both physical and emotional force.

St. John 3:16 is a familiar passage of Scripture that reads, "For God so loved the world that He gave His only begotten Son, that whoever believes in Him should not perish but have everlasting life." God the Father loves us so much that He sent God the Son to die in our place. He was rejected and humiliated; He suffered, bled, and He died for us that we might gain eternal life. Christ submitted to the Father willingly, out of love and obedience to God. He "pleased" God by submitting. He trusted God and submitted. Through Christ's submission not only can one be reconciled back unto the Father but also Christ is exalted. He sits on the right hand of the Father. We are to be like Christ and emulate His attributes. So, submit. Submit to God. Submit to one another. If there is a trust issue between you and your mate because one of you violated the other's trust or because of past baggage that was brought into your marriage from prior relationships, I suggest that you find a good Christian counselor to help you work through your issues. I also suggest that you both pray about the issue and allow God to grace you to overcome.

Ephesians 5:21–33 reads:

> Submitting to one another in the fear of God. Wives, submit to your own husbands, as to the Lord. For the husband is head of the wife, as also Christ is head of the church; and He is the Savior of the body. Therefore, just as the church is subject to Christ, so let the wives be to their own husbands in everything. Husbands, love your wives, just as Christ also loved the church and gave Himself for it, that He might sanctify and cleanse it with the washing of water by the word, that He might present it to Himself a glorious church, not having spot or wrinkle or any such thing, but that it should be holy and without blemish. So husbands ought to love their own wives as their own bodies; he who loves his wife loves himself. For no one ever hated his own flesh, but nourishes and cherishes it, just as the Lord does the church. For we are members of His body, of His flesh and of His bones. "For this reason a man shall leave his father and mother and be joined to his wife, and the two shall become one flesh." This is a great mystery, but I speak concerning Christ and the church. Nevertheless let each one of you in particular so love his own wife as himself, and let the wife see that she respects her husband.

Remember that charity begins at home. Sometimes people can be patient everywhere but at home. Learn to be more patient with your spouse. There's no need to snap at everything or take things out of context. Be gentle and kind. Be long suffering and forbearing. Be more tolerable.

Keep in mind that two unique personalities have come together to become one and be patient with one another. You can never be exalted without humiliation, which is freedom from pride and arrogance. You must have humbleness of mind, which includes a modest estimate of one's own worth. This means putting aside the attitude that would want to say, "I'm grown"; "He/she is not my boss"; "He/she is not going to tell me…" Listen. Come to a "meeting of the minds" and go on. Wife, you must submit to your husband. He has the responsibility of leadership of the family. Husband, you must submit to the needs and concerns of your wife. Her opinions, concerns, needs, and feelings are important too.

Women, you were created to be a helpmeet to your husband. Men, women are not man's subordinate. God is the head. The husband is to be the leader of the family, but it must be done in love, with gentleness, and with the consideration of your wife and your family's needs being your priority. Consideration meaning everything is not to be one-sided, with the same person always getting their way and being satisfied while the other one is constantly giving in; but consideration meaning many times putting your wife and family's needs ahead of your own wants. It's giving a mature thought, a balanced thought, a considerate thought to decisions with some serious deliberation!

Submission is not always easy; in fact, true submission is exhibited when you don't feel like doing it. You know, "I'm not feeling it" but you do it anyway. We've all felt like not doing something from time to time, but giving in and doing the right thing shows maturity and growth. It's the right thing to do when you tell your mate where you're going and give a time frame of your return. It's the right thing to do when you want to make a large purchase out of the joint account but you discuss it first with your mate and come into agreement, not just say, "This is my money" and purchase it. It's the right thing to do when you want to go on a prolonged fast that you run it past your mate and the two of you agree (it's now his or her body too).

Learning how to submit to your mate also brings accountability to one another. You are accountable to your mate and he or she is accountable to you. This can help you to avoid infidelity. Be cautious about spending private time with someone other than your mate because it leaves opportunity for the devil to bring division into your relationship. Think before you do something. Invite your spouse to work gatherings. If you must have a meeting with someone of the opposite sex, bring a third person if possible (especially if you know this person is attracted to you or vise versa). I know most would like to think that they have "it" in control. But bonds can develop when two people spend time together and if you position yourself in areas where temptation can enter, your flesh and your body can or will respond accordingly. Examples include boss with secretary; coworkers; pastors or leaders with members, etc. It may start out innocently and end up in an affair.

Matthew 26:41 reads, "Watch and pray, lest you enter into temptation. The spirit indeed is willing, but the flesh is weak." I know you want to do right. I know you love your spouse. But if we put our flesh in the wrong place at the wrong time it leaves one in a precarious position to temptation. Watch were you go and what you do. Watch who you spend time with. Be careful and be accountable to your mate. Cover yourself and your marriage covenant by not putting yourself into such predicaments, even to the point that you care about how it may appear to the outsider or your spouse even in the face of pure innocence. Think before you do something. Would you like it if your spouse did the same thing—would it be OK? Is this something that's appropriate for a godly married person to do?

To keep one's focus in perspective, remember that submission is "because of." When we submit to God it is "because of": because He's God; because He loves us; because He has our best interest at heart; because we want to please God; because we trust Him; because we love Him. And out of our love for Him, we submit. In a marriage you should submit to your mate because he or she is your life partner; because he or she loves you; because he or she is supposed to have what's best for the union at heart; because you are supposed to trust your mate. And out of the love you have for your partner, you submit. This is not always convenient. This is not always what you're feeling at the present time. Many times you won't be "feeling" it, but think about it. Will it benefit the union? Will it promote harmony in the union? Just submit. Matthew 7:12 reads, "Therefore, whatever you want men to do to you, do also to them, for this is the Law and the Prophets."

Tips:

- Men: Love your wife as Christ loves the church. Honor and cherish her. Make her feel special and loved.

- Women: Respect your husband. He is the head of the house. Make him feel respected and loved.

- Men: Listen to your wife's opinions and ideas.

- Women: Don't go head to head with your husband.

- Submit to one another

Chapter 6
Assignment

1. Each of you write down three areas in which you have trouble submitting to your mate.

2. Each of you write down three areas in which your mate has trouble submitting to you.

3. Each of you discuss your own problem areas with your mate.

4. Each of you discuss your mate's problem areas.

5. Discuss how to implement change for all twelve problems and follow through with the implementation.

*Use effective communication skills. Be cordial and loving.

Chapter 7

CHILDREN AND FAMILY

THIS CAN BE a really sensitive topic but it must be addressed. We are living in times that are much different than biblical times. The generation of today is bolder than prior generations. There have been sayings like, "It's your thing, do what you wanna do," "It's my prerogative," and "I'm a grown man/woman," to name a few. Even children have a spirit of wanting their way and wanting to do what they want, when they want. Some of the children are saying, "You're not the boss of me" and similar sayings. The mind-set that says, "I can do what I want" has assisted in affording the world to be in a promiscuous state. Thus when a man and a woman "tie the knot" they sometimes have children from a previous relationship or relationships. This can be difficult on a marital relationship. I will discuss this briefly within the confines of this book, but for in-depth information, Christian counseling would be advised, especially if it is causing issues or stress in your marriage.

Children are a very important part of marriage. The dynamics of the union changes when children enter the mix. It changes from the major focus being on the couple's

73

needs and broadens to the family's needs. As parents, you will soon learn to put your children's welfare and needs before your own.

It is the plan of God that we "be fruitful and multiply." It is beneficial to the kingdom of God that we raise up godly offspring who will reverence, love, and serve God. When having children, it is important to love them and raise them up according to godly standards. It's also good to plan and have family time weekly. Plan things that all of you can enjoy together, but understand that the activity should be geared especially toward the children's enjoyment. Family time will be appreciated by the children and yourselves, and it is what making memories is all about. It will also influence them and teach them the values of spending quality time with their children.

This topic should actually be discussed in detail before marriage, but since this book is for the individuals after making the marriage vow, it will be broken down in two major parts. First I want to address the couple without any children. You should discuss with your mate whether the two of you want to be parents. There are factors to consider like age, health, finances, and so forth. If so, discuss how many children you want. Discuss topics like parenting techniques. You will find that one may believe in corporal punishment and the other wants to use a more lenient approach such as "time out" or "taking privileges" for wrongdoing. Talk about this in advance, as it may be a problem down the line. Give hypothetical situations and try to get on the same page with your parenting strategies. Get an understanding of your mate's upbringing and viewpoints about raising children. This is going to be crucial, as it will most definitely affect how he or she will raise your children.

Next I want to deal with the couple with children from another relationship. This is a little more difficult and sensitive, but necessary to address due to the fact that it is highly prevalent in the times in which we're living. Again, this should have been dealt with prior to marriage, as it could create a lot of issues. The two of you should come to terms regarding boundaries—boundaries with discipline, and boundaries with the children's fathers or mothers.

How are you going to handle the baby's dad's/mom's relationship with your spouse? What will your role be in the parenting, finances, discipline, and so on? I know you may not see that as a problem now if you're new in your marriage, but I've been doing Christian counseling for over seventeen years, and believe me…it usually is a problem. Couples argue over the financial responsibility of the children. They get in conflict about disciplining the children. The children get above themselves and play the natural parent against the stepparent. It can become stressful and divide the relationship. Don't allow this to happen in your relationship. Talk with one another. Determine the role of the stepparent. Will they be permitted to discipline the child, or is disciplinary action just the duty of the biological parent? Never allow the child's momma or daddy drama to come in between your relationship. The baby's momma's or daddy's opinion should never outweigh your spouse's opinions and feelings. There should be a strong stand of unity between the two of you if your union is going to work and last.

Personally I believe that you should not have married someone you don't trust. This means you should trust them to love you and yours. Trust them to love your children like their own. With this being said, you both need to come up with agreeable terms regarding the children to make your marriage work. Everyone's marriage is different and everyone's terms will be different. Just come up with what works for your union and work it. If you try something for a while and it doesn't seem to be working, don't be rigid to the point that you won't change. Make adjustments to the terms until you find what works for both of you.

Understand that every individual has different upbringing, and regardless of how similar the two of your upbringings may objectively appear, they are different. Some were raised in homes with both their parents; some raised in a single parent home; others by grandparents or another form of a family. Some homes experienced a lot of love, some didn't. Some people believed in showering their children with outward affections of love, others didn't. This is why it is important to get an understanding of your mate's ideas of parenting and come into agreement.

Proverbs 22:6 reads, "Train up a child in the way he should go, And when he is old he will not depart from it." Parenting is an awesome task for the believer. God entrusts us to raise up the next generation of believers; the next generation of mighty warriors for Christ; the next generation of virtuous women and men of valor. God has entrusted the believer to raise up a next generation that can perform acts of destruction against the kingdom of darkness and fulfill God's kingdom purpose. That's an awesome responsibility!

Lastly, before you bring children into the mix, make sure your union is happy and stable enough to endure the challenges that parenting will bring. Understand that having children doesn't cement a relationship that's already in crisis; in fact, it adds stressors. Get through your major issues first before adding an innocent, vulnerable being to your union. Children need your love and affection. They too want to feel like they're a part of the union…family. Give them what they need but understand that they also need to see a harmonious marriage between their parents. They want to see the two of you love each other. So when children enter the picture, always make time for just the two of you to keep the relationship happy and healthy. Children are a huge responsibility and they will change the dynamics of the marriage, but they add to it so much joy and love!

TIPS:

- Try to be in agreement in front of your children.

- Even though you are a couple, remember to make your children feel loved and special.

- Enjoy your children; they grow up so fast.

Chapter 7
Assignment

1. Discuss if you want children and how many. Some of you may already have a child or children from prior relationships, so discuss if you want to have additional children to add to your union.

2. If you answered yes to question 1, when will procreation begin? Are you financially ready now, or what is the projection of when you will be? Is your union stable enough to include a child or children?

3. Sometimes fate happens during labor and delivery, making it necessary for a couple to make a decision between saving the life of the spouse or the life of the child. This is very traumatic and unfortunate. Discuss each of your viewpoints of this hypothetical situation.

4. Both of you write at least three hypothetical questions regarding rearing a child. (Examples: Do you believe in corporal punishment? What do you think about time out for toddler misbehavior vs. corporal punishment? What is your opinion on taking away a preteen or teen's privileges vs. corporal punishment?)

5. Discuss with your mate the hypothetical (in some cases real issues) questions regarding child rearing.

6. Reach agreeable terms.

7. Discuss how to start a college fund for your child or children.

8. If you have children, plan a family outing or activity to be done this week. Try to incorporate family time weekly or bi-weekly.

Chapter 8

GROWING AND CHANGING

THE MARITAL UNION begins with the honeymoon stage, where everything is blissful. This is the stage where the relationship is fun and loving. Usually faults go unnoticed or are of little to no concern. But as time goes on and the honeymoon stage is faced with the challenges of life and the personalities of one another surface at another level, the couple must learn to do things to enrich their union and their love for one another. They must learn to accept that they each have faults and that no one or nothing is perfect. The couple must learn to accept that bliss is not the norm but that it, along with the rest of the relationship, must be worked on. One must understand that things change but your love and devotion to one another should not only remain, but also deepen. You must learn how to take your relationship from the surface honeymoon blissful love to a mature deeper intimate level of love and bliss.

Your union goes through numerous stages and you must make adjustments for every stage in order to keep the union blissful. Too many times couples assume that since they are no longer feeling the "heart flutters" they used to feel for their mate, they are no longer "in love" with their mate.

79

They are misled by the illustration that society portrays of a loving relationship. When looking at love in the movies and on televisions, it is usually portrayed as passionate with hot sexual tension. With everyday stress and situations you will realize that movie love is not reality love. Every day will not be filled with passionate, hot love. Most people are not happy and upbeat all the time due to life's circumstances that can weigh one down, but that doesn't mean you're not still in love; it just means it's changing.

It's important to know that with time comes change—change in your relationship with God; change in your personal life; change in your marital relationship; change in you. Everything evolves, it's inevitable. These changes don't mean you love your spouse any less; in fact, your love for one another should deepen and grow. It just means there's a change. It's important that you acknowledge the change but then make adjustments to mature and grow together in every aspect of your relationship. Everyone grows and change is inevitable both on the personal level and as a couple. One grows from experiences that he or she encounters and from the challenges and issues of life.

Understand that growing and changing is a natural part of life. It is important that you not allow this natural part of life to allow the two of you to grow apart but rather grow together. Spend quality time together. Date your mate. If possible (and you should make it possible), schedule a weekly date night. It doesn't have to cost a lot, it just has to be something that the two of you enjoy doing together. It is also important that everyone has and keeps individual interests. This is what makes you, you. This is what expands your mentality. This is what helps you to grow and not become stagnant. Being stagnant can put a damper on your relationship.

Gaining new information and implementing it, whether

it is spiritual information, educational information, job-related information, etc., gives a person a sense of self-worth. It makes you feel good about yourself when you learn and implement information. Knowledge is good! Broaden your horizons both individually and as a couple. As a couple, you can attend mutual recreational activities like a class together at a gym, or a class together at a home store to renovate something in your house. Whatever the case, look for things to do where the both of you can grow together and stay connected. Share some of your daily experiences that you encounter with your spouse. For example, you can discuss something that happened on your job, with the children, and so forth. Pray together. Learn godly principles and grow spiritually together.

Growing and change is different for everyone. Some resist change. Some embrace change easier than others. It is easier for a person to adjust to change and grow when the person introducing the change uses positive tactics as opposed to negative ones. In other words, don't nag or beat someone down because they're a little slow to change and grow. Try to avoid harsh words at all costs, but rather compliment the change and growth that they're displaying. Reward them with compliments. Reward them with love tokens (something they like) for their change.

Life consists of constant changes and it is important that one learns to adapt. If there is no change there is no growth. If there is no growth there is no life. The circumstances of life have a way of changing individuals. We all have decisions to make as to how we allow things to change us. You can allow things to change you for the good or the bad according to your willingness to submit to the Word of God. When life's stressors peak, one must not allow their emotions, their reactions, or their actions to be guided by their flesh, but be guided by the Word of God. Always monitor your reactions by the Word of God not on your emotions. Emotions can sometimes get you into trouble.

Be willing to change and not hang on to things that didn't work in the past. Sometimes people get stuck in behaviors and are unwilling to let go and try what the Word of the Lord says. Don't get stuck. Don't be afraid to change. Don't be slow to grow. Try something new. Try new things with your mate. Try new godly behaviors. I believe it is the will of the Lord that marriage be enjoyable, fun, loving, and till death do us part. I don't believe God intended for His people to be in unhealthy, unhappy marriages. I believe this occurs when people refuse to allow God to be the center of their marriage and either one or both of the individuals refuse to change and grow.

We are seeing a high divorce rate in the secular world as well as in the church. I'm contributing this to the fact that many people have a problem with changing. Either they are not willing to change or don't know how. Some don't see a reason to change. They feel like they're all right the way they are. In any event, I say change is good. Nothing stays the same. Just as seasons change, people change and relationships will change. A good relationship must adapt and adjust to changes. God wants us to change and mature. A relationship will benefit from individuals changing and maturing for the better. Don't allow your union to become routine. Routine can breed boredom and taking one another for granted. Strive for changing and growing personally and as a couple.

Tips:

- Time and life change people and things.

- Change is good.

- Don't be afraid of change…embrace it!

CHAPTER 8
ASSIGNMENT

1. Both partners list at least three things you've been refusing to do that your spouse wants to do.

2. Think about how you can implement them into your relationship.

3. Each of you share your list with your spouse.

4. Discuss how they can be implemented and make sure it is agreeable to both of you.

5. Schedule a date night and follow through.

Chapter 9

FINANCES

FINANCE IS A very important part of the marital relationship. It is a topic that should be discussed in detail before the tie is completed. It is also a topic that many couples omit from the conversation. Know that money issues are some of the main reasons for the high divorce rate. Everyone has different values and ideals about how money should be handled and this can cause a tremendous strain on the marriage.

Finances should be discussed prior to the marriage to get a mutual understanding of one another's perspective about money, spending trends, and saving ability. The financial stability of the union is predicated on the ability of the couple to work together toward common financial goals.

It is also wise to be informed of your partner's credit score. I know most of you were so in love that the topic of credit scores did not arise but I have counseled numerous couples over the years, and believe me, if not now, somewhere down the line it will be an issue. A good credit score determines and separates the renter from a homeowner. Being able to save determines your ability to go on nice vacations, and your ability to save for a down payment on your first home or the ability to upgrade to another a home. Being financially responsible separates one from being in debt to creditors versus paying cash for what you want or at least being able to pay off the debt in one or two payments.

Money is important to every union and you must understand that you must be responsible with what God gives you! You should live at a level that is responsible, not overextended. Pay debt responsibly. Not only does this increase your credit score but it also speaks of your character. It is not biblical to make a debt and not repay it. Romans 13:8 reads, "Owe no one anything except to love one another, for he who loves another has fulfilled the law." You can't praise over unpaid debt that you're trying to ignore, meaning you can't act indifferent to someone you owe or get mad because they want what's due them. Repay what you borrow. Pay off your debts. If you're a born-again believer you should not overextend yourself to the point that you are unable to give God His 10 percent.

Malachi 3:8–11 reads:

> "Will a man rob God? Yet you have robbed Me! But you say, 'In what way have we robbed You?' In tithes and offerings. You are cursed with a curse, For you have robbed Me, Even this whole nation. Bring all the tithes into the storehouse, That there may be food in My house, And prove Me now in this," Says the LORD of hosts, "If I will not open for you the windows of heaven And pour out for you such blessing That there will not be room enough to receive it. And I will rebuke the devourer for your sakes, So that he will not destroy the fruit of your ground, Nor shall the vine fail to bear fruit for you in the field," Says the LORD of hosts.

If you're struggling financially, pay your tithes and experience the blessings of the Lord at another level. If you can't give the entire 10 percent, consistently give what you can and work your way up. For those of you who thinks tithing ended in the Old Testament, Luke 18:12 reads, "I fast twice a week; I give tithes of all that I possess." Tithing was practiced in the Old and the New Testament and it is still relevant for the believer today. In addition to paying your tithes, you should be able to pay your entire household expenses and still have 5 percent but preferably 10 percent (or more) to put into a savings account. My definition of a savings account is not an account where you put money in to use the ATM card for purchases, but an account that goes untouched for your future. It can later be used to assist you in accomplishing long-term goals or for an unexpected emergency.

The day and time that we live in requires two people working together to fulfill a common goal and to live comfortably. Whether both individuals work outside of the home or only one person is bringing home income, you both must work together. This means that the two of you must set financial goals and both individuals should be adhering to them. Make a budget. Stick to the budget. Some couples split the budget 50/50 while others divide the bills or choose other agreeable terms. There are no set rules; just determine what works for your union and work that. Keep in mind, however, that no one wants to work and not have any personal money. Therefore, make sure your budget arrangement takes this into account so that you each have your own personal spending monies.

Both partners need to fulfill their obligations to render their share toward the budget. This means that regardless of how you may be feeling on payday, you release your portion toward the budget. Even if you've had some type of disagreement with your mate, you release your portion. Even if you see an outfit you want, you release your portion. Even if you feel like you'll just die if you don't get those shoes, you release your portion—you won't surely die! Funny! We're living in a society where a lot of the time it takes two paychecks to live comfortably; therefore, both individuals must be willing to work together at all times to meet their goals.

Evaluate your financial expectations and make sure they are realistic. Unrealistic expectations can put you into insurmountable debt. This can cause stress and strain on the marital relationship. For example, if your income together is $50,000, you should not be living at the $100,000 level. Everything should line up with your income. Don't get it twisted—I'm not saying don't trust God; I'm not saying don't believe God for nice things. I'm saying it doesn't make sense to get a brand new Mercedes Benz when you live in an apartment. It doesn't make sense to be riding in a Lexus when you don't have a garage to put it in. First Corinthians 14:40 reads, "Let all things be done decently and in order." Do things "decently and in order"—not to be seen by men, not to keep up with the Joneses, but in wisdom—and keep within the parameters of what makes your union financially comfortable not financially stressed.

Come to an agreement with the financial budget. It's not fair for one person to carry the load while the other does what he or she wants with "his or her" money. Remember, the union should come first. It's not fair for one to be stressed with responsibility while the other splurges on whatever, wherever, whenever they want. How much do you really love your mate if you can look at him or her and allow him or her to be stressed without you trying to pull your weight? It is not fair for one to be stressed while the other is walking around blessed. Stress in the marriage induces frustration, which over a period of time becomes anger, which if not corrected can turn into bitterness. Bitterness can cause your mate to resent the source of their stress…you! This can destroy a marriage! I know that there are some relationships where only one paycheck is sufficient to meet the needs of the household expenses, but there are other ways to work together. Learn how to not be an overspender to help with the budget. Learn how to buy groceries but still save money. Learn that you don't need to purchase everything that you see and like. Try purchasing things on sale instead of paying full price.

When you are dealing with finances, remember that you are both unique individuals coming together from different backgrounds with different attitudes and perspectives about spending and saving. You have been shaped by your parents' or guardians' viewpoints of saving and spending. You have been conditioned by previous relationships how to spend and what to spend on. Your own wants and needs play a significant role in your spending and saving. You must talk to your mate and get an understanding regarding their value of money. Don't be judgmental because your mate is as unique as yourself. Find out what they determine as "needs" versus "wants." Be open and share your views as well and then come to a mutual agreement about what can be curtailed and what is an actual "need."

This is extremely important because every couple should have a plan for saving and a savings account to show that they're serious. A guideline would be to save 10 percent of your income monthly. If this is not presently doable, start with 5 percent or whatever you can afford. There should be a savings for short-term and long-term goals. Short-term goals could be to save for a vacation or trip that you both want to take within a year. Long-term goals could be for large purchases such as a car, house, or renovations to your house or starting your own business within the next four to five years. Saving is crucial. You should always have something for a crisis or rainy day.

Good communications is the key to successful financial harmony. You must get an understanding of one another's perspective about finances. You must come to an agreement on a budget. You both must keep the budget and respect the other's feelings. Don't walk around looking blessed while your mate is walking around looking stressed. OK, so you're twenty-one-plus-plus, but if you want to purchase a large item it should first be discussed with your mate and an agreeable decision should be made. If you have to hide your purchase, something's wrong. Don't come home with it and feel justified because "I work hard for my money." The money is no longer "mine" but "ours." If you have to hide and/or justify what you buy, something's wrong! Communicating about money is essential. This chapter may not be as long as some of the other chapters in this book, but don't get it twisted—money matters are extremely important. In fact, financial issues are some of the leading causes of divorce, so talk with your mate about finances. Be open. Be honest. Be agreeable. Be *one*.

TIPS:

- Agree on a budget.

- Your money becomes one…our money.

- Don't be blessed while your mate is stressed.

CHAPTER 9
ASSIGNMENT

1. Make a budget for your household expenses.

2. Separate "wants" from "needs" as many of the "wants" may have to be deleted to effectively save.

3. Agree on how much each of you is going to contribute to the budget…and stick to it!

4. Discuss a realistic savings plan and start one. Put it in writing.

5. Discuss a mutual financial short-term goal. This should be something you both want to see happen within the next eight to twelve months. (Examples: vacation; purchase a new car; new furniture etc.)

6. Discuss a mutual financial long-term goal. (Examples: purchase a home; save enough to start you own business, etc.)

Chapter 10
SEX

S EX IS A topic that a majority of Christians believe should not be discussed. Sensuality and sex is often looked upon as a carnal topic or taboo for discussion. People tend to think it's just "something" that's done in a Christian marriage, without the understanding that it's "something" that requires learning your partner's wants, needs, and desires. It too requires "work" to keep the passion and fire blazing! Talking about sex or sensuality is extremely controversial, especially in the church world, but a visual observation of the Christian dynamics will reveal that sexual indiscretion is ramped in the church. Religious idealism would prefer to keep sexual topics undiscussed, but sexual sins become an open reality when someone's sexual needs are not being met in their marriage. I've seen where someone doesn't share with their mate what they need from their mate because they don't want to seem "unspiritual" or carnal, but then they go and get their needs met outside of the marriage. Statistics report that approximately 50 percent of marriages end in divorce and infidelity is a leading cause. So I believe this is a crucial topic to explore.

Not only is infidelity reigning in the secular world, but it is also prevalent in the church. It may "seem" like not discussing sex or one's needs makes you appear more "spiritual" and less carnal, but the truth of the matter is God Himself ordained sex, and sex is a very vital element of the marital relationship. Sex is the "icing on the cake" of the marital relationship. The activities of daily living and the stress that comes along with life can deplete one's spirit, but having sex with your spouse brings rejuvenation. It's the euphoria that ties the two of you together and helps to keep the bond between two people unbreakable. Sexual physical release is an innate drive and need. It's not dirty. It is ordained by God. It's not lustful to desire your mate. It is ordained by God. Sex is the glue that binds things together. It is the adhesive that binds the husband and wife together in an intimate bond when they are entwined in ecstasy, giving and receiving pleasure from their lover, their spouse. It's the physical act of intimacy where the "two become one."

In the day and time in which we live, permissibleness prevails and most individuals' marital relationship is not their initial relationship. Many have also experienced a sexual encounter or encounters with someone other then their marital partner. Unfortunately this behavior brings with it additional experiences, hang-ups, thoughts, drama, and appetites that play a role in your present relationship with your spouse. This is one reason why it is important that the husband and wife discuss as well as practice sexual intimacy. This gives them an understanding of one another's wants, needs, and preferences.

Song of Solomon 4:12 reads, "A garden enclosed Is my sister, my spouse, A spring shut up, A fountain sealed." Know that it was not the will of God for man and woman to experience the bonding of the flesh with anyone other than their mate, but with the fall of man came the indulgence of every fleshly pleasure. It's just another area of sin that man has to deal with. Wouldn't it have been easier if man had just obeyed God? If this were done, there would not be so many "soul ties"; soul ties with one person while in a relationship with another, remembering how that person made them feel while they're in a relationship with someone else, and in some cases longing for someone else and constantly comparing their present partner to their "soul tie."

When God ordained the marital union, He designed man and woman to fulfill every one of the other's needs. Sex is the glue that holds the relationship together. Sex is also effective in reducing tension and stress. When everything around you seems to stress you out, you still have the arms of one another to find physical comfort and gratification in. First and foremost, sex is ordained by God. It binds two people together in a physical act where they truly become "one" in the flesh when engaging in intercourse. It is spiritual because it deepens the love for your partner, which strengthens the bond and works as a deterrent of extramarital affairs.

Physically, sex is an innate desire. There is a desire in every human being for sexual gratification or a sexual release. Sex is also an emotional need. It feels good to be wanted and desired by your mate. It makes one feel wanted and needed. During the climax of the sexual act the body releases oxytocin and endorphins. Endorphins are noted as pain relievers and some studies have shown that they can relieve headaches and some women's menstrual cramps (pain usually only relieved briefly). The oxytocin gives a euphoria that improves ones mood, meaning someone is happy, and happy people make happy relation-ships. Sex is also considered exercise; the act itself burns calories, which can lower or help reduce one's weight and also assist in lowering blood pressure. It can also help to give one a good night's sleep.

It is important to tear down the "religious" mind-set that thinks sex should not be discussed because it makes you appear "carnal," and realize that sex and infidelity are running rampant within the church as well as the secular world. It is important that the needs of both individuals be met. It is important to understand that sex is not only for procreation, but that it is fun and to be pleasurable for both the man and the woman. As previously men-tioned, everything that I address is based on biblical prin-ciples with St. Matthew 7:12, the golden rule, being highly emphasized: "Therefore, whatever you want men to do to you, do also to them, for this is the Law and the Prophets."

If you want your spouse to pleasure you, you must be willing to pleasure him or her. If you want to be gratified and satisfied, you must be willing and able to gratify and satisfy your mate. If you want to experience an orgasm, your mate most likely wants to experience one too…I'm just saying. Know that men and women are different. They are just wired that way; but this is not a problem. It just takes patience, knowledge, understanding, and communi-cation to be able to pleasure your mate.

First, understand that no two individuals are the same. Therefore, what worked in the past with a prior partner may not work with your mate. This means you may have to unlearn old techniques and learn techniques that work for your spouse. If this is your first, great! You're getting a fresh start. In both instances you must learn your mate. Also realize that men and women differ in that men are visual and women usually take a little longer to turn on. Women, since men are visual beings, play it up! Look good. Put on what you know attracts him. Men, women like it when you seduce them…so do it. It's in a man's nature to hunt and conquer, which means he's creative enough to catch his prey. Catch your woman with your seductive skills and conquer what you want!

With men, just looking at your wife in sexy lingerie may turn you on, but women require foreplay. Foreplay is verbal, emotional, and physical. Verbally stimulate her mind. Tell her how good she looks. Tell her you only have eyes for her. Tell her how she makes you feel. Emotionally build her up. Foreplay doesn't just begin in the bedroom but should happen throughout the day with the most important and final phases being done by the husband to the wife's body and by the wife to her husband's body prior to and during the actual sexual act. Physical foreplay is important to most women. Caressing and kissing your mate is an important part of the equation that should be savored, not rushed. Find out what he or she needs and don't be shy about participating. Find out what type of lingerie he wants to see you in and wear it for him. Find out what she wants to see you in and wear it for her. Your mate chose you. He or she loves you. He or she desires you.

Another area in which men and women differ is that most men are into the "number" or quantity and most women tend to focus more on the quality. Make your intimate times together count, whether it's a leisurely romantic encounter or a loving "quickie."

First Corinthians 7:1–5 reads:

> Now concerning the things of which you wrote to me: It is good for a man not to touch a woman.

> Nevertheless, because of sexual immorality, let each man have his own wife, and let each woman have her own husband. Let the husband render to his wife the affection due her, and likewise also the wife to her husband. The wife does not have authority over her own body, but the husband does. And likewise the husband does not have authority over his own body, but the wife does. Do not deprive one another except with consent for a time, that you may give yourselves to fasting and prayer; and come together again so that Satan does not tempt you because of your lack of self-control.

This passage of Scripture clearly defines the intent for sexual relations between a husband and a wife. First it acknowledges that sex is an innate desire. Second it informs that outside of the marriage it is immoral and a sin. Next it concludes that sex in a marital union should be with the intent to totally fulfill each other's needs.

The Bible tells us that the husband is to "render to his wife the affection due her, and likewise also the wife to her husband." The husband and the wife are to submit to one another and render sexual gratification to one another. This denotes the wife meeting the husband's sexual needs as well as the husband meeting the wife's sexual needs. When this is accomplished it decreases Satan's ability to afflict the union with infidelity.

Know that you and your spouse should be able to communicate about all topics. This is a topic that you should be able to discuss with your spouse. Communicate effectively and share your likes and dislikes with your "life mate." Most people are not mind readers, so how will they know what you want, what you like, and what turns you on, if you don't communicate it to them? They need to know what turns you on and what turns you off. They need to know how many times a day or week you need sex from them. They need to know what to do to satisfy you. They need to know if they are satisfying you. Every individual is unique and what worked for a prior partner may not necessarily work for this partner. Therefore, learn to communicate effectively. Don't belittle your partner. Don't tear them down. Don't shut them down. Just be loving and honest and share what each of you likes and dislikes. To take the tension out of the situation you can take turns with each of you sharing a like and a dislike. Make sure to phrase it so that it's not offensive; for example, "I like it when you…" or, "You turn me on when you…" Avoid statements like, "You've been doing this and it's not working for me…" and, "All you think about is yourself…" Instead of putting your mate down, build him or her up. Tell them what you like and encourage them to continue doing it without being overbearing or hurting his or her feelings. If you're shy about voicing what's turning you on, try moaning when they're doing what you like or gently moving their hand or body part where you need it, or position your body appropriately.

Here are a few tips for sex in marriage, and keep in mind they are all based on the Word of God:

1. It is to be continuous. Rarely do libidos match, and if not addressed this could lead to infidelity. Again I know this is Christian teaching but I need to address this because sexual indiscretions and affairs are happening in the church. Every marriage is not equally yoked. Some married before they got saved. Some married someone who wasn't saved. Some married someone who was a carnal believer, confessing salvation but not obeying or partially obeying godly principles. Many are married and

believers but keeping "parts" of themselves, not allowing God to deal with them and make them whole. They only allow God to operate in certain areas of their lives. So it is important to deal with libidos and the issues it can cause. It would be great if the married couples' libidos were in sync, but most of the time the couple's individual sex drives are different. Discuss your particular situation and compromise. There is no number that is a specific guide to the times per week, just a number that is specific to your unique union. Therefore, it is important that this be discussed and specified by both of you and compromise be made to adjust so that the person with the strongest libido is "covered." You "cover" your mate when you are meeting his or her needs so that you don't leave him or her open to Satan's infidelity attacks. For example, if one of you desires sex every day and the other desires once a week, compromise somewhere in the middle. Maybe every other day would suffice. Be open and understanding to your mate. Don't get mad if their desire is stronger than yours. Don't get mad if their desire is less than yours. Remember, you still love this person and you don't want to offend them. Compromise. Marriage is all about giving and taking. Marriage is all about negotiating and coming to an agreeable solution. Fidelity is included in your marital covenant; therefore, it is your responsibility to meet the needs of your mate in bed.

2. You are not to withhold sex as a bargaining tool. Verses 4 and 5 of 1 Corinthians chapter 7 explain that your body is no longer your own. The wife no longer has "authority over her own body" and the husband no longer has "authority over his own body." Do not use sex to try and get what you want in the relationship. It should not be withheld because you are mad. It should not

be withheld because you didn't get your way earlier that day. Keep in mind you can draw more flies with honey as opposed to drawing them with vinegar. Be sweet and kind to one another. Keep in mind that the sexual experience binds couples together and is the designated physical act for the "two to become one" physically. Lovemaking is the perfect time to unwind together and bond. It also opens the door for free verbal communications in the "afterglow" of sharing your love. This scripture also means you don't have the right to say "no." If you're mate is sick, that's understandable. But if they have a headache every day, that's something else. Maybe they'd better go get a physical to make sure they're OK, or you'd better talk with your mate to make sure everything's OK with your union. You have to submit to meeting your partner's needs. God made man and woman and we were designed to meet the needs of our mate.

3. First Corinthians 7:3 informs us that sexual relations are to be equal and reciprocal. Both parties are to be satisfied. It is easier for the male to obtain his climax but it takes a little more work for the female to achieve an orgasm. Find out what she needs and likes and help her to enjoy an orgasm. Wife, find out what your husband likes. I base all my teachings on the golden rule:

> Therefore all things whatsoever ye would that men should do to you, do ye even so to them: for this is the law and the prophets.
>
> —MATTHEW 7:12, KJV

If you don't want to be left without receiving a sexual release, don't leave your partner that way. This leads to frustration. And it can lead to the partner not desiring sex with you because they are not being satisfied. If not corrected it can lead to frustration, which turns to anger, which leads to resentment and if not rectified, bitterness. Each is to give the other what he or she needs. You were perfectly designed by God to fulfill the needs of your mate. Please know that although you've given the authority of your body to your spouse this does not mean that the spouse has permission to inflict pain or degrade your body. You are to love and respect your spouse's body as you do your own! With that being noted, enjoy and pleasure one another!

Hebrews 13:4 reads, "Marriage is honorable among all, and the bed undefiled; but fornicators and adulterers God will judge." You are to meet the sexual needs of your spouse according to biblical parameters. Spice up your marriage with romance or being romantic. Romance is simply using your imagination to do something out of the ordinary and something extravagant for your love. It's something they normally wouldn't expect, but it's a pleasant surprise. It may "normally" seem corny but it brings a smile to your partner's face. It makes their day.

On a side note, romance is not sex but it can lead to it! Also understand that foreplay and sex don't just happen in the bedroom; they start way before you get there. It can be little suggestive notions throughout the day. It can be a sexy phone call or text message that one partner makes to another. It can be little flirtatious ways. Use your imagination and have fun.

The marital bed is honorable. It is highly regarded by God. It is to be respected by both parties and each is to treat the other fairly. One person should not be pleasured and the other frustrated. Keep the sparks ignited. Because you're a believer doesn't mean you have to allow sex to become routine. Be a participant, not just a recipient. Be open to trying different times of the day; try different rooms; try different positions; try different or new techniques; pull out the candles and make an aroma bath for two.

Personal hygiene is important! Bathe or shower for the experience (unless it's a spontaneous encounter). Make your intimate sexual encounters special. Women, pull out your sexy lingerie, because men are visual beings. Men, dress for the occasion also. Always try to look good for your man or woman. Don't become predictable and routine with the same time of day, the same way, same room, same position, etc. Try a new haircut or hairdo. Dress so that you look good. This will appease your mate in and out of the bedroom. Buy cologne or perfume that your mate likes. If he or she wants to see you in a specific romantic item, wear it for them—after all, he or she is the one you want to turn on and keep turned on and attracted to you. Remember, sex was ordained by God. Sex is meant to be good and pleasurable. Sex is a natural, pure act of love with your spouse. Sex is to be fun…it's not that serious. Be playful and loving. This is a time for the playful side of you to be expressed.

Sex is not something to be viewed as dirty or something that you are not to discuss with your mate. Talk about your likes and dislikes with your mate. This is where your communication skills will have to kick in! Some people are shy when it comes to talking about their sexual desires and needs. Some are less experienced than others and are not sure of what they need to help them achieve optimal pleasure to bring them to a climax. Some just assume that their mate is supposed to "know" what they need; never assume, always share your needs with your mate!

Remember, don't be judgmental as your mate shares his or her desires and needs.

Side note: Being judgmental can be expressed nonverbally as well as verbally. Therefore, be aware of your body and facial expressions as your lover expresses him or herself (this applies to every area of communication). One's posture speaks a million words, so if you want your mate to continue to open up to you, don't judge or be impatient with him or her verbally or nonverbally. Be patient and listen attentively. Try sharing in an atmosphere that is conducive for intimate conversation as opposed to rushing the topic in an inappropriate place at an inappropriate time. Remember not to criticize your mate, but make your requests and needs known in a non-threatening, non-judgmental manner. Try sharing on date night when it's just the two of you. A neutral place would be suggested.

The human mind is a complex organ that allows one to associate things. We can see something and associate it with good or bad, with a pleasant or unpleasant occurrence. Therefore, if you're discussing sexual issues that may become "opinionated" and turn into a hot topic, you may not want to discuss them in your favorite romantic spot or the bedroom so as not to taint that spot with unpleasant memories. If you choose to give suggestions in the bedroom it may be better received if you gently guide your partner. This can easily be done by verbal clues or body positioning (putting what you need where you need it as long as you're not forceful and your mate is receptive). Positioning or aligning your body can also be subtle ways of suggestion.

Men and women are wired differently. It is easier for men to achieve orgasm but it takes a little more for a woman. Men and women have different needs. They are turned on differently. They require different stimulation for pleasure and orgasms. On a side note, there are some informative instructional materials available that are not porn. Some of the teachings are Christian oriented and not offensive and may bless your marriage. The information can and will assist you in avoiding routine sex, which may become boring, and assist you in keeping your sex life hot and passionate.

Keep in mind that sexual dissatisfaction leads to less sex. The person who's not being gratified will not want or desire to participate in the act. If the problem goes unresolved feelings can progress from frustration to anger to bitterness. This can evolve into extramarital affairs or divorce. I know this is Christian teaching but realistically speaking, "I'm just saying," the divorce and extramarital affair rates are as high in the church as they are in the secular world. So I must keep it real! If you don't address a sexual area that needs to be addressed, you leave yourself or your mate uncovered and you leave open access for the devil to gain entry into your marriage.

Genesis 2:25 reads, "And they were both naked, the man and his wife, and were not ashamed." There should be no shame in your sexual game with your spouse. It is sanctioned by God. It is a covenant bond between a husband and a wife. Allow your sexual relationship with your spouse to bind you two closer together in intimacy. Allow it to take your love and devotion for one another to another level. Have an open mind and explore new levels of intimacy with your companion, your friend, your lover, your partner—your spouse. Enjoy!

TIPS:

- The sexual act is important and should be consistent and mutually gratifying.

- Personal hygiene is imperative for both parties. Make your mate feel special and bathe or shower for the occasion (unless it's spontaneous).

- Be sensitive to his or her needs; learn and know their likes and dislikes

CHAPTER 10
ASSIGNMENT

1. Both of you share three things with your mate that turns you on.

2. Both of you share at least three things with your mate that you dislike.

3. Have sex in a different place that you mutually agree upon.

4. Try something different that is agreeable to both of you. There should be one thing from each of you. Try what he or she wants tonight. The next time it will be the other's turn.

5. If possible, plan a romantic night or weekend for just the two of you and follow through.

Chapter 11
LOVE AND TRUST

SOMETIMES INDIVIDUALS HAVE the tendency to confuse lust with love. According to Webster's dictionary lust is defined as, "to have carnal desire; to desire eagerly the gratification of carnal appetite; longing desire." First John 2:16 reads, "For all that is in the world—the lust of the flesh, the lust of the eyes, and the pride of life—is not of the Father but is of the world." Lusting and being in lust is not of God but of the world. God is love. Showing love and being in love is of God.

I know most people are initially attracted to someone by their outward appearance, and it is natural to be drawn into wanting to be with someone because of this, but as a believer we must not walk in the flesh but in the spirit.

Galatians 5:16–21 reads:

> I say then: Walk in the Spirit, and you shall not fulfill the lust of the flesh. For the flesh lusts against the Spirit, and the Spirit against the flesh; and these are contrary to one another, so that you do not do the things that you wish. But if you are led by the Spirit, you are not under the law. Now the works

of the flesh are evident, which are: adultery, fornication, uncleanness, lewdness, idolatry, sorcery, hatred, contentions, jealousies, outbursts of wrath, selfish ambitions, dissensions, heresies, envy, murders, drunkenness, revelries, and the like; of which I tell you beforehand, just as I also told you in time past, that those who practice such things will not inherit the kingdom of God.

Love is more than a physical attraction. Love is more than physical pleasure and gratification. Love is of God.

Love, as defined in the dictionary, is "an affection of the mind excited by beauty and worth of any kind, or by the qualities of an object which communicate pleasure, sensual or intellectual; to regard with affection, on account of some qualities which excite pleasing sensations or desire of gratification. In short, we love whatever gives us pleasure and delight."[1] This is natural love, but godly love is the total opposite. Godly love is not superficial. It requires one to give more of him or herself then they may get in return. It is a selfless love. Godly love loves someone as you love yourself. In some cases this can be a problem because there are some individuals who don't love or know how to love themselves. In this case a good Christian counselor is advised. In most cases, individuals love themselves. We must all work on sharing and giving selfless love.

Matthew 22:36–40 reads:

"Teacher, which is the great commandment in the law?" Jesus said to him, "'You shall love the LORD your God with all your heart, with all your soul, and with all your mind.' This is the first and great commandment. And the second is like it: 'You shall love your neighbor as yourself.' On these two commandments hang all the Law and the Prophets."

First and for most know that God is love and if you are a believer you are to emulate the attributes of God. God is all about love.

First John 4:7–9 reads:

> Beloved, let us love one another, for love is of God; and everyone who loves is born of God and knows God. He who does not love does not know God, for God is love. In this the love of God was manifested toward us, that God has sent His only begotten Son into the world, that we might live through him.

Secondly, love is a commandment of God. He commanded His people to love one another, not lust one another. He gave a commandment that every born-again believer must obey.

Know that love is a choice. Everyone must make a conscious decision to accept or reject Christ and salvation. Everyone makes a conscious choice to obey or disobey the Word of God and godly principles. You must make a decision to love your mate and work on staying in love with your mate. You must make a choice to try and make one another happy. You must make a choice to try and get along with one another. You must make a choice to grow together as opposed to becoming distant. You must make a decision to try to sexually please and gratify one another. You must make a choice to either use old techniques to communicate that didn't work in the past, or change your communication techniques to new ones that work. You decide effective communications or ineffective communications; make the relationship work and be happy or keep the marriage in constant agitation; stay together or drift apart; great sex or mediocre or bad sex.

The commandment of God is to love. I believe the home is to be a place of refuge; therefore, it should be a home of love, two people working together to make one happy lifestyle. It is a choice that you and your spouse must make and obey as followers of Jesus Christ.

Ephesians 5:25 reads, "Husbands, love your wives, just as Christ also loved the church and gave Himself for it." Men, you are to love your wives as Christ loved the church. He loved the church to the point that He gave Himself for it. Christ gave His all for the church—for you and me. What are you giving of yourself for your wife? Are you giving the "me," "mine," and "I" away for "us," "we" and "our"? Are you dominating or negotiating?

Realize too that when Christ gave Himself for the church, not all gave an appropriate response to Him. Some accept Christ as their personal Savior, some don't. Some totally commit to Christ, some don't. Nevertheless, He freely gave of Himself and He freely gives to us. God makes provisions for us, provides for us, protects us, heals us, keeps us and loves us. And even as believers we still find in many instances that we are not always obedient to Him and deserving of His affections. Yet He continues to shower us with mercy because of grace.

This should be manifested in the marital relationship as well. Men, sometimes you may feel as though your wife has offended you, angered you and in some instances "dissed" you. Nevertheless, you must continue to shower her with your love and affections. As a husband you must learn to freely give to your wife. Give your time, emotions, attention, body, and affections. Show her you appreciate what she does for you. Token gifts every now and then are nice…flowers, candy, perfume, etc. for no reason are always appreciated. Something that tells her you thought about her today. It doesn't have to be expensive and break the budget, it just needs to be something she likes. Never get so complacent that you take her for granted. Verbally tell her what she means to you. Verbally express your appreciation for what she does.

Ephesians 5:22 reads, "Wives, submit to your own husbands, as to the Lord." Don't let the times we live in and the hype of a diva influence how you treat your man. Your man wants your love and your respect. Even as you don't try to play a "diva" with God, don't take it over the charts with your husband. That gets old and tired fast!

Women, you must learn never to go "head to head" with your man. This is hard for some and harder for others, but it is the will of God that you respect your man. Be conscious of how you treat him, especially in public. Many times there are some things you can say and ways you can act behind closed doors, if done appropriately, but in many instances these same behaviors are not appropriate in public. Don't disrespect or belittle him. Learn how to give a soft-spoken response. Learn to make suggestions and get your point heard without nagging. Nagging is not becoming. You can push him away with constant nagging.

Show him you appreciate how he handles his business, meaning you, the children, the household, and how he takes care of things. Verbally compliment him. Normally women give of their time and emotions, so add onto it your attention, body, affections, and respect. A token gift for no reason every now and then is nice—cologne, candy, a CD, etc.—something that says I thought about you today.

It doesn't have to be expensive; it just needs to be something he likes. Submit to your man as he submits to God.

Galatians 5:22–25 reads:

> But the fruit of the Spirit is love, joy, peace, long-suffering, kindness, goodness, faithfulness, gentleness, self-control. Against such there is no law. And those who are Christ's have crucified the flesh with its passions and desires. If we live in the Spirit, let us also walk in the Spirit.

It's not all about you. Consider your partner's feelings, desires, dreams, wants, and needs. Realize that love also means being vulnerable to one another. It's an opening of your heart to another person knowing that there's a possibility of being hurt (we're all fallible), but freely and openly loving them enough to be vulnerable to them anyway. Being vulnerable to someone can be difficult but it is necessary for taking your love and intimacy from one level to another level. Let me say, however, that this cannot be done without truly trusting someone.

Trust is defined in the *Webster's Dictionary* as "confidence; a reliance or resting of the mind on the integrity, veracity, justice, friendship or other sound principle of another person." You must trust the "sound principles" of someone else to the point that you feel comfortable enough to commit your feelings, heart, life, and care in the hands of that individual—your spouse. That's deep!

Trust is an issue. People have problems trusting God; that's why many only partially commit to Him. Some say they're fully committed to God but they keep areas of themselves to themselves. They don't allow God to enter into certain compartments of their lives. They don't allow God to deal with and change certain parts of them. Many have trust issues. In the spirit and one's walk with God, it is important to totally and completely trust God. Your relationship with God will not go to the next level until you learn to walk in a deeper level of love and intimacy with God. Trusting God should be in faith. But most humans have the "Thomas belief/faith/trust," which makes it hard to just do it. But in order to walk in a level of intimacy with God and to be all that God has ordained for you to be, you must learn to just trust Him, knowing that He's God and has your best interest at heart. So then most of man's trust develops out of his relationship with God. The deeper your intimacy level is with God, the more you trust Him. You learn His attributes. You fellowship with Him. You learn His Word. You learn His character. Your trust and love for Him deepens. So it is in the marital relationship. Your trust for your mate is developed over time as you get to know them, as you learn that they adhere to godly standards the more you let down the guards to your heart and open up to your mate. You gauge how they lovingly treat you and you let down your guard a little more. Trust is learned and earned. One learns to trust their partner as their partner earns their trust.

Because of the diversity of individuals and the different phases of marriage that individuals may be in who are reading this book, I would be remiss if I didn't at least touch on distrust due to human error. Everyone is prone to error and sometimes the errors may cause distrust to erupt in your relationship. Some may be dealing with errors that have caused distrust in your relationship. Such errors as gambling, repeated disruptive cycles, pornography, sexual indiscretions, physical and/or mental abuse, and additions can hinder or terminate trust.

Understand that the act brought a breach to your

covenant and that it's going to take time to repair the situation, if it's repairable. The person who caused the mistrust needs to be patient. It's going to take time for you to re-earn the trust of your mate. You should not demand their trust just because you said, "I'm sorry." The offender must bump their demonstration of love, for their mate and marriage, up another level. The offender must make him or herself accountable to their mate in every area, such as giving them access to you cell information, computer passwords, and everything else you kept secret. Inform your spouse where you're going and with whom. You must become transparent and open to your spouse. You must be accountable to avoid entering into and succumbing to the same error or errors. Both of you must be willing to work on building, re-building and re-establishing the trust.

Understand it will not happen overnight; it's going to be a process. This is going to take time. This is going to take patience. This is going to take much prayer! Many times a good Christian counselor is necessary to help both of you navigate through the process and to help you to deal with your feelings. Don't be embarrassed to seek the help that you need to get through the issues and put your marriage back on the right track.

Trust is vital to a viable marital relationship. Trust can take a relationship from incomplete to complete honesty. Trust takes superficial communication to intimate communication. It's easier to share your innermost heart with someone you can trust. It's easier to submit to someone you trust. You know they have your best interest at heart and it's easier to be vulnerable to that person. Vulnerability allows a person to show their inner softer, loving side. One can stop acting hard and being on guard like they're in the presence of the enemy, and expose more of their loving side.

Trusting will improve every area of the marital union. It will improve the financial aspect of the union. It is easier to release your money in a union where there is trust. Parenting will improve. Sex will improve. You will find that it's easier to express yourself more intimately in the bedroom with someone you trust intimately. Submission will be less of an issue because you trust your mate to love you, not control you.

Love will deepen because of that trust bond. Communication will improve. Your mate will feel more at liberty to discuss everything with you at a deeper level. Keep in mind, however, that it is important that once your mate confides something in you that you are not to use it down the line against them. God doesn't do this to us. Don't use a weakness they confessed to you against them in an argument or disagreement. This will cause the trust to diminish. Guard their trust in you like it is your heart on the line, because the two of you are one. What hurts your spouse, what concerns him or her, what affects him or her…hurts, concerns, and affects you.

Another thing about love and trust is the importance of always being open and honest with your mate. Through my years of dealing with couples I have noticed that in many cases one person is oblivious to the depth of a relationship problem, or they don't realize that there is even a problem. Sometimes one individual feels like "all is well" because his or her needs are being met, or because he or she doesn't have any more expectations than what they are already receiving and giving, therefore they are totally unaware of their mate's discontentment. This is a serious issue. Sometimes the one who is discontent holds these feelings in or shares them with the wrong person. This can lead to looking for companionship outside of the marriage, which at times leads to extramarital affairs.

It is imperative for each of you to share your feelings with your mate. If you need something that you're not getting from your mate, tell him or her. If you're unhappy about something in the relationship, tell him or her. If you're getting bored—or are bored—tell him or her. Don't let your silence bring severance to your relationship. Don't allow your silence to make you seek companionship outside of your marriage. Don't let your mate believe that all is well, when in your mind it's not! Share with your life partner in love, using good communication skills, not to hurt him or her but to bring change in the area where it's needed. Many times you will find that they too would like to do some things differently but was a little awkward about bringing it up. Be open, your mate is looking to you and trusting you with their heart for your honesty and love.

First Corinthians 13:4–8 reads:

> Love suffers long and is kind; love does not envy; love does not parade itself, is not puffed up; does not behave rudely, does not seek its own, is not provoked, thinks no evil; does not rejoice in iniquity, but rejoices in the truth; bears all things, believes all things, hopes all things, endures all things. Love never fails.

Life can be hectic with all of the things we have to do. But one must balance their daily activities so that they always make room for their mate. Prioritizing is a must. Things must be done in order. God first; marriage and family second; then ministry, jobs, and careers. God is interested in your marriage. God wants there to be love in your marriage. Charity and love begin at home, and then spread abroad. Balance and prioritize the activities of daily living so that you keep love alive in your marriage and home. Make your mate feel special and loved daily. Remember his or her birthday and make it his or her special day. Show your love to your mate by remembering and celebrating your anniversary and holidays in ways that will be special for the both of you.

First Peter 4:8 reads, "And above all things have fervent love for one another, for 'love will cover a multitude of sins.'" When dealing with one another you must remember that love will cover a multitude of faults. No one is perfect—not even you—but godly love will cover a multitude of faults. In other words, don't be so focused on your partner's faults and shortcomings. We can all find faults in someone or something, but don't get stuck there. Strive to look at their positive traits. Strive to love each other unconditionally.

When you took your marriage vows you vowed to love your mate. You made a conscious decision to make a commitment with your spouse. You made the choice that "this" is the "one." Now you must make the conscious decision to work on keeping love alive.

> Beloved, let us love one another, for love is of God;
> and everyone who loves is born of God and knows
> God. He who does not love does not know God, for
> God is love.
>
> —1 JOHN 4:7–8

Understand that no one remains in the honeymoon phase of any relationship perpetually. The honeymoon phase is usually when you're still euphoric about your mate. Everything is "new" and good. You're "high" on love for your mate. Conversation is good. Sex is good. Finances are usually not a focused problem. You just love, love, love him or her. But after the honeymoon comes the reality of life and life's circumstances and issues. Now you also see his or her idiosyncrasies but you still must choose to continue to love him or her.

Time is going to change your mate. Many will evolve into more mature individuals with more diverse interests. This is why it's vital that you grow with your mate. Life is going to change your mate. The outward appearance as well as some parts of his or her personality will grow and change. She may gain weight and certain body parts may droop and sag. He may gain weight or become bald. It's important to remember that physical outward appearances change, but love and commitment prevail. That's why it is important to make a core connection in every way possible with your spouse. Remember, however, it's still important to look the best that you can and "work" what you're working with. Women, change your hairstyle and give him something "new" to work with every now and then. Men and women, continue to dress fashionably. Both partners keep up with your personal hygiene. This is important. You must show that you care about yourself and your mate by caring about your looks and personal hygiene. It is not appealing or desirable to be with someone who doesn't care about their presentation. What you did to win him or her you must continue—and then some—in every area of the relationship.

You still have to love, but on another level; a deeper level that comes from knowing, communicating, connecting, and loving your mate; a love that comes from the heart. Don't allow love to become a commitment to one another without passion for one another. Don't allow love to become complacent without attraction. Don't let your love wane…keep love alive!

TIPS:

- It's easier for a woman to submit to a man who she feels loves her totally.

- Don't try to physically force someone to submit; rather, love them into submission.

- Love means making "us" as a couple work and putting "us" before "I/me."

CHAPTER 11
ASSIGNMENT

1. Both of you make a list of at least five things you love about your mate.

2. Both of you share the list with your mate.

3. Both of you give considerable thought to and list at least one area to work on, to become more vulnerable to your mate.

4. Both of you discuss with your mate the area of vulnerability that he or she listed and talk about ways to assist him or her to overcome their hesitancy. This will not happen overnight. It's going to take time and patience.

5. Both of you give your mate at least two compliments.

6. Both of you give thought to and come up with at least one thing to do for your mate to show your love and appreciation for him or her. Follow through by doing it.

Chapter 12

IT'S NOT THAT SERIOUS

A merry heart makes a cheerful countenance, But by sorrow of the heart the spirit is broken.
—PROVERBS 15:13

PROVERBS 17:22 READS, "A merry heart does good, like medicine, But a broken spirit dries the bones." Many times some people take things too seriously. Marriage is a serious commitment, but it is also meant to be fun and loving. Don't take everything so seriously. It's OK to laugh. God intended for His people to laugh. Learn to make jokes and laugh with one another. It's not that serious, even if there's a dilemma "right now." You can get through it.

You will have dilemmas, maybe even some drama from time to time. Issues and disagreements will surface, but don't take them to the top. Don't allow every disagreement to escalate into an out-of-control debate. If it's really not that important to you but more important to your mate, it's OK to concede and give in. Conceding doesn't make you a weaker person, it makes you understanding and flexible. Many times being a person who is able to concede denotes a person who's open to adapting and changing, which represents growth. A person who's changing and growing denotes maturity. Understand that a person who adapts, changes, grows and matures is a person who is an asset in a marital relationship and a gem to the kingdom of God. If the same person keeps conceding, however, this could be a problem. Marriage is a give and take, not the same party giving and the same one always taking. Learn to pick your "fights" (cordial disagreements) wisely. Think, how important is this to me? Is it worth wasting time arguing or debating when we could be spending this time more wisely? It's really not that serious.

Learn to laugh together. Laughter lightens the situation. Try not to take everything so serious. Life's too short. Be happy. Laughter has spiritual benefits. Laughter has medical benefits. It has been medically documented that laughter can increase the blood circulation, which can assist in preventing hardening of the arteries. This is good for the heart. If a problem or issue arises, always focus on the problem, not the person. Don't allow your feelings and emotions to escalate to the point that you react in a way that is contrary to the Word of God. You cannot govern someone else's actions, but you can govern your reactions and actions in response to theirs. In other words, don't allow your mate to make you act or react contrary to the Word of God. It's not that serious.

TIPS:

- Practice laughing at trivial issues as opposed to turning the molehill into a mountain.

- Agree to disagree without being disagreeable.

- Life's too short. Be happy.

CONCLUSION

IN CONCLUSION WORK, work, work! It takes a lot of persistent, consistent work to keep love alive in a relationship and deepen the love and bond of a marital union. I believe that the majority of married couples want to remain married to each other. I also know that circumstances of life, dealing with issues, financial pressures, and the rearing of children, can cause a relationship to become fragile. Time can cause the marriage to become secondary to everything else. It can cause you to take your partner for granted. This should not happen. This will not happen if you continue to put one another as your priority.

You must constantly work on developing and maintaining your relationship in a state of blissful harmony. To believe that the marital union will remain blissful perpetually on its own is hopeful thinking. The marriage can be blissful but it takes work. The marriage can remain blissful but it takes work. Remember the union is a coming together of two individuals from different backgrounds. You both have different upbringing. You both have had different experiences. No two individuals are exactly the same. There will be different desires, different drives, different goals, different ideals, and different ways of doing things, but they can all work together for the good to give greater dynamics to the relationship. "Variety is the spice of life." Learn from one another. Be open to one another's input into the marriage.

Both partners must be willing to work on building a tie that's not easily broken. In the center and at the foremost of the tie should be Christ. Allow God to deal with every area of your life, including your marriage. He can deliver you from unwanted baggage, if you let Him. It is the will of God that marital ties be "…until death do us part." The climate of society has proven anything but this as we note the high divorce rate—secular as well as in the church. Some people are using the marital union as a trial and error period. They try it on for "a minute" and if it doesn't "work" they quickly end the relationship…this is not the plan of God. Individuals must realize that every relationship requires work because it is made up of fallible people.

Most people believe that in order to succeed in anything requires effort. To be promoted on one's job requires that the individual put effort into doing the very best that he or she can so that their work exceeds the efforts of the other candidates for the same promotion. They understand that they must learn and grow to succeed. Being promoted in the church requires diligence and effort as well. It requires a giving up of one's self; sacrifice, dedication, and discipline. So why is it that most people are striving and putting effort into everything else except their marital relationship? It takes work! It takes diligence. It takes dedication. It takes both individuals being committed and in many cases it will take some attitude adjustments. Also strive not to allow your marriage to become routine, which breeds boredom. Boredom can be an opening for the attack of the enemy in your marriage. Mix it up with something new every now and then.

Commitment is a term that is loosely used today. People "commit" but renig when it's "not working for them." Most people want to do what they want when they want. Slang and lyrics to songs have be accepted as the rule to self-pleasing as opposed to self-giving. Slang like, "It's your thing do what you want to do," "It's my prerogative," "I'm a grown man or woman," "I'm twenty-one-plus-plus," and "You're not the boss of me" have been adopted to relieve men and women of their responsibilities of commitment and accountability. The age that we're living in and this generation are finding it more difficult to make commitments and keep them. But if you've taken that leap into marriage; if you've jumped over the broom; if you've made a vow of until death do us part—it is your duty to commit to working to make the relationship work. It is your duty to commit to loving your spouse. It is your duty to commit to making one another happy.

Everyone should understand that just like God expects us to change to better our relationship with Him, we must be willing to change to better our relationship with our spouse. An unbending, uncommitted, non-giving, selfish partner can be a deal breaker of the union. I'm not propagating divorce; I'm just stating what happens. I'm keeping it real!

Everyone differs in their spiritual conviction levels. Individuals differ in their walk and devotional level with God, meaning many will not remain in a relationship where they are no longer "feeling" it. They will not stay where they no longer feel happy or fulfilled. People can only tolerate their needs not being met for so long and everyone's tolerance level is different. Are you willing to test your partner's tolerance level? Are you willing to forfeit a loving, fulfilling relationship because you're unwilling to put work into your marriage?

Understand that a severed relationship does not happen overnight. It's progressive. It happens when things are not worked on. It happens when issues are not addressed and corrections are not made. It happens when frustration turns to anger and anger to resentment and resentment to bitterness. Everyone has a breaking point. Everyone has a point of no return; that's why the divorce rate is so high…just keeping it real. Are you willing to change and make adjustments in your relationship to keep love alive? Are you willing to work on keeping communication open and effective? Are you willing to work to keep the passion aflame?

This book was written to give insight with simplistic instructions to assist in navigating through and avoiding unnecessary drama in your marriage. By all means, if your marriage needs help, don't allow pride to stop you from seeking counseling from a neutral Christian counselor or spiritual leader. Marriage is meant to be happy. The relationship is supposed to be fun. The two of you are supposed to be best friends. The two of you are supposed to be lovers. Give God access and include Him in every area of your marriage…don't exclude Him. Don't be selective, separating areas of your life from God, but allow God to heal you in every area of your life so that you can be the best person and mate that you can be. This includes allowing God to heal you of past hurts and pains as well as past issues and past experiences. Allowing God to rule and reign in you personally and as a union is what will make your marriage successful, happy, blissful, harmonious, passionate, loving, and healthy. Allowing God to rule and reign in every area of your life is what will take your marital union from ordinary to extraordinary.

Operate by the "golden rule." Matthew 7:12 reads, "Therefore, whatever you want men to do to you, do also to them, for this is the Law and the Prophets." Treat your mate the way you want to be treated. Respect your mate the way you want to be respected. Love your mate the way you want to be loved. Don't allow the cares and issues of life to separate what "God has joined together." Enjoy one another in every way!

> Father, in the name of Jesus, I pray for the individuals reading this book. I pray that they receive these simple instructions and that they don't just read them but that they apply them to their marriage. Give them the grace to change. Grant them the grace to implement change. Give them the grace to adjust. Teach them to love and trust one another at another level. Break the strongholds in their lives personally so that they can truly become one with their mate. Allow their marriage to fulfill the destiny that You've ordained for their union. In Jesus' name, I decree and declare that no union that You have put together shall be broken. Let them experience love, trust, passion, and bliss in their marriage at another level in Jesus' name. Amen.
>
> BE BLESSED!
> PASTOR SHARLENE

NOTES

CHAPTER 11: LOVE AND TRUST

1.   *Merriam-Webster's Eleventh Collegiate Dictionary* (Springfield, MA: 2003).

ABOUT THE AUTHOR

Dr. Sharlene F. Fullwood co-founded Jubilee Evangelistic Ministries Inc. and Nehemiah Community Development Corporation in Coatesville, Pennsylvania. She has been pastoring at Jubilee for more than seventeen years alongside her husband. She is the mother of one daughter named Destine'. Sharlene has a heart for marriages and the Lord has used her to facilitate unique Marriage Enrichment Seminars. She has been doing Christian counseling for more than seventeen years and holds a master's degree in Christian counseling, which she received from Christian International School of Theology. Sharlene is a prayer intercessor, a prayer warrior, and she operates in the fivefold ministry as a gifted prophetic minister under a powerful breaker anointing ministering deliverance and healing into the lives of the people.

CONTACT THE AUTHOR

If this book has been a blessing to you, please look for my other books:

God Reveals His Glory In the Earth

Before the Two Become One

Additional copies of this book available at:
Jubilee Evangelistic Ministries Inc.
920 E. Lincoln Highway/ P.O.BOX 1534
Coatesville, PA 19320
610-380-9601